Financial Longevity
Through the Sweitzers' Eyes
Most People Have Accumulation Strategies but
Very Few Have Tax-Efficient Income Strategies

Ken Sweitzer,
with Cari Sweitzer
SWEITZER INCOME PLANNING, LLC

SWEITZER INCOME PLANNING, LLC
18 Lyme Street
PO Box 747
Old Lyme, CT 06371
Book layout ©2019 Advisors Excel, LLC

Financial Longevity Through the Sweitzer's Eyes/Ken Sweitzer.—1st ed.

ISBN 9798654468246

"It is not necessary to do extraordinary things to get extraordinary results."

~ Warren Buffett

"History is still being written. You're writing it every day. The wheels still spin, and what you do or what you don't do will be a part of it. You build a legacy, not from one thing, but from everything."

~ Oprah Winfrey
2018 USC Commencement Speech

Table of Contents

Planning in Any Environment

As we were wrapping up the final touches to this book, the COVID-19 pandemic had just started to disrupt the world.

Today we are sheltered at home with two of our three grown children as there are talks about things opening again.

We were shocked to find the most powerful country in the world, The United States of America, was not prepared enough to simply supply personal protective equipment for our hospitals and first responders.

Then we heard how the novel coronavirus is mainly affecting the elderly, age sixty and above, and those with underlying health conditions. I was incredibly surprised that, having celebrated my sixtieth birthday in June, I'm now elderly.

Now more than ever it is important to get a full perspective of your financial situation to prepare for uncertain financial and lifestyle changes that we know too well have and will occur.

As we send this book to publication, we are reconfirming something that has been our core belief all along: It is more important to have a complete plan instead of a few volatile portfolios. We are helping people realign their risk for growth with principal protection to avoid future losses.

We have built our business on helping clients prepare for both positive and challenging landscapes in order to enhance their retirements and protect against perils that could derail them.

Stay safe, stay healthy, start planning, and enjoy this book.

The Importance of Planning

Have you ever received a telephone call that completely changed your life? I did. My phone call came in October, 1978. It was my freshman year of college. I was two weeks into the semester at the University of Connecticut. My football coach walked into my dorm room and told me I needed to call my mom as soon as I could. I immediately found the nearest payphone on campus and dialed my mother's number.

As soon as I heard her voice, I knew something was wrong. She began telling me all kinds of details about my father's family business. None of the details were making any sense. My mom was panicking as she spoke. I said, "MOM . . . stop talking for a minute, you're not making any sense. What's going on?" She then told me the bank had repossessed our family home, the house we had grown up in. My divorced mom and my two younger brothers had to move out immediately.

You see, my dad took over his father's business years earlier, but, despite him being a hard worker, my dad didn't know how to effectively run a business. He got behind on the bills and the taxes of the business, and, soon after that, he stopped paying the mortgage on our home. You see, my dad was part of a very proud generation. It was hard for men to ask for help back then. Maybe it was a sign of weakness to them. What my dad needed was someone to give him sound financial advice, but that advice never came.

I left school, left my team, and hitchhiked home that Tuesday. I remember it as if it were yesterday. Walking down my driveway, I saw my brothers, my mom, and a couple friends carrying all our belongings into the front yard. I remember feeling that empty pit in my stomach. I felt so helpless. I helped them move in with friends. I returned to school that Friday and met with my advisor the next week to change my major to finance.

My mom and brothers lived with friends before moving from one rental to another through the following years. We all pitched in every month to try to make ends meet. That lack of financial knowledge and communication devasted me and changed the lives of my entire family. My mom worked hard but was not able to earn enough money to be self-sufficient.

I knew I would never allow myself to go through a terrible situation due to the lack of information like this. Forty-one years ago, I turned a defining event in my life into my career. What I believe to be the wisest book ever written says, "for the lack of knowledge, people perish." As you may know, that phrase is referring to eternal things, but the same can be true for people who don't have financial knowledge. I want to share some of that knowledge with you in this book.

CHAPTER ONE

Longevity

Y ou would think the prospect of the grave would loom more frightening as we age, yet many retirees say their number one fear is actually running out of money in their twilight years.[1] This fear is, unfortunately, justified, in part because of one big factor: We're living longer.

According to the Social Security Administration, in 1950, the average life expectancy for a sixty-five-year-old man was seventy-eight, and the average for a sixty-five-year-old woman was eighty-one. In 2020, those averages were eighty-three and eighty-eight, respectively.[2]

The bottom line of many retirees' budget woes comes down to this: They just didn't plan to live as long. Now, when we are younger and in our working years, that's not something we necessarily see as a bad thing; don't some people fantasize about living forever, or at least reaching the ripe old age of one hundred?

However, with a longer lifespan, as we near retirement, we face a few snags. Our resources are finite—we only have so much money to provide income—but our lifespans can be

---

[1] Samiha Khanna. Journal of Accountancy. February 14, 2019. "Clients' Top Fear: Running out of Money."
https://www.journalofaccountancy.com/news/2019/feb/top-retirement-fears-201920387.html.
[2] Social Security Administration. 2011 Trustees Report. "Actuarial Publications: Cohort Life Expectancy."
https://www.ssa.gov/OACT/TR/2011/lr5a4.html

unpredictably long, perhaps longer than our resources allow. Also, longer lives don't necessarily equate with healthier lives. The longer you live, the more you will likely need to spend on health care, even discounting long-term care needs like nursing homes.

You will also run into inflation. If you don't plan to live another twenty-five years but end up doing so, inflation at an average 2.5 percent will raise your $50,000-per-year budgeted need up to $93,000 per year. Or if you live another eight years as inflation rises, you will need about $810,000 to cover those same expenses.[3] And this is before you count the expenses of any potential health care or long-term care needs.

Of course, we don't necessarily get to have our cake and eat it, too; our collective increased longevity hasn't necessarily increased the healthy years of our lives. Typically, our life-extending care is most widely applicable to the part of our lives where we will need more care, period. Think of a pacemaker at eighty-five, or cancer treatment at seventy-eight.

"Wow, Ken," I can hear you say, "way to start with the good news first."

I know, I've painted a grim picture. But all I'm concerned about here is the cost. It's hard to put a dollar sign on life, but that is essentially what we're talking about when we're talking longevity and your finances. According to the Stanford Center on Longevity, more than half of pre-retirees underestimate the life expectancy of the average 65-year-old.[4] Those low estimates leave a lot of time unaccounted for. Living longer isn't a bad thing; it just costs more, and one key to a sound retirement strategy is preparing in advance for that expense.

One woman I know illustrates this picture perfectly. Her mother passed away in her late seventies after years of suffering

---

[3] Katie Brockman. The Motley Fool. August 19, 2018. "More Americans are Living into Their 90s—and That's Bad News for Their Savings." https://www.fool.com/retirement/2018/08/19/more-americans-are-living-into-their-90s-and-thats.aspx.

[4] Stanford Center on Longevity. "Underestimating Years in Retirement." http://longevity.stanford.edu/underestimating-years-in-retirement/.

from Alzheimer's disease. Her father died at eighty from cancer. With modern medicine and treatment, this woman survived two rounds of breast cancer, lived with diabetes, and relied on a pacemaker, extending her life to age eighty-eight, nearly a decade beyond what she anticipated. However, she and her husband had saved and planned for "just in case," trying to be prepared if they had to move, or they needed nursing home care, or they needed to help children and grandchildren with their expenses. One of their just-in-case scenarios was living much longer than they anticipated. The last six years of her life were fraught with medical expenses, but she was also blessed with knowing her five great-grandchildren and deepening relationships with her children and grandchildren. She was able to pay for her own medical care, including her final two years in a nursing home, and her twilight years were truly golden.

From age eighty-five to eighty-eight, she was more socially active, with many visits from family and friends. She participated in more activities than she had in the seven years since her husband died. Her planning from decades earlier allowed her to pass on a legacy to her children when she passed away herself. The legacy she left behind can be measured both in dollar signs *and* in other intangible ways.

Living longer may be more expensive, but it can be so meaningful when you plan for your just-in-cases.

Retiring Later

Planning for a long life in retirement partly depends on when you retire. While many people end up retiring earlier than they anticipated due to injuries, layoffs, family crises, and other unforeseen circumstances, continuing to work past age sixty and even sixty-five is still a viable option for others and can be an excellent way to help establish financial comfort in retirement.

There are many reasons for this. For one, you obviously still earn a paycheck and the benefits that go with it. Medical coverage and beefing up your retirement accounts with further savings can be significant by themselves, but continuing your income also should keep you from dipping into your retirement funds, further allowing them the opportunity to grow.

Additionally, for many workers, their nine-to-five job is more than just clocking in and out. Having a sense of purpose can keep us active physically, mentally, and socially. That kind of activity and level of engagement may also help stave off many of the health problems that plague retirees. Avoiding a sedentary life is one of the advantages of staying plugged into the workforce, if possible.

I know people who retired in the late nineties after a good run in the market. They felt as if they had enough money to last their entire lifetime, but they kept the majority of their retirement investments at risk in the stock market. The sudden market decline in the aughts of the new century reduced these folks' retirement income by over 40 percent. When you are taking income from volatile investments, you don't always get your principal back, and your income could decrease—in some cases as much as 40 percent. Many of these retirees were left with the unfortunate circumstance of having to return to work to replace their lost retirement income.

Health Care

Take a second to reflect on your health care plan. Although working up to or even past age sixty-five would allow you to avoid a coverage gap between your working years and Medicare, that may not be an option for you. Even if it is, when you retire, you will need to make some decisions about what kind of insurance coverage you may need to supplement your Medicare. Are there any medical needs you have that may require coverage in addition to Medicare? Did your parents or grandparents have any inherited medical conditions you might consider using a special savings plan to cover?

These are all questions that are important to review with your financial professional so you can be sure you have enough money put aside for health care.

Long-Term Care

Longevity means the need for long-term care is statistically more likely. If you intend to pass on a legacy, planning for long-term care is paramount, since it's estimated that nearly 70 percent of Americans will need some type of it.[5] However, this may be one of the biggest, most stressful pieces of longevity preparation that I encounter in my work. For one thing, who wants to talk about the point in their lives when they may feel the most limited? Who wants to dwell on what will happen if they no longer can toilet, bathe, dress, or feed themselves?

I get it; this is a less-than-fun part of the process. But a little bit of preparation now can go a long way!

When it comes to your longevity, just like with your goals, one of the important things to do is sit and dream. It may not be the fun, road-trip-to-the-Grand-Canyon kind of dreaming, but you can spend time envisioning how you want your twilight years to look.

For instance, if it is important for you to live in your home for as long as possible, who will provide for the day-to-day fixes and to-dos of housework if you become ill? Will you set aside money for a service, or do you have relatives or friends nearby whom you could comfortably allow to help you? Do you prefer in-home care over a nursing home or assisted living? This could be a good time to discuss the possibility of moving into a retirement community versus staying where you are, or whether it's worth moving to another state and leaving relatives behind.

These are all important factors to discuss with your spouse and children, as *now* is the right time to address questions and concerns. For instance, is aging in place more important to one spouse than the other? Are the friends or relatives who live nearby emotionally, physically, and financially capable of helping you for a time if you have an illness?

---

[5] Moll Law Group. 2019. "The Cost of Long-Term Care." https://www.molllawgroup.com/the-cost-of-long-term-care.html.

Many families I meet with find these conversations very uncomfortable, particularly when children discuss nursing home care with their parents. A knee-jerk reaction for many is to promise that they will care for their aging parents. This is noble and well-intentioned, but there needs to be an element of realism here. Does "help" from an adult child mean they stop by and help you with laundry, cooking, home maintenance, and bills? Or does it mean they move you into their spare room when you have hip surgery? Are they prepared to help you use the restroom and bathe if that becomes difficult for you to do on your own?

I don't mean to discourage families from caring for their own; this can be a profoundly admirable relationship when it works out. However, I've seen families put off planning for late-in-life care based on a tenuous promise that the adult children would care for their parents, only to watch as the support system crumbles. Sometimes this is because the assumed caregiver hasn't given serious thought to the preparation they would need, both in a formal sense and regarding their personal physical, emotional and financial commitments. We can't see the future: Alzheimer's disease and other maladies of old age can exact a heavy toll. When a loved one gets to the point that he or she is at risk of wandering away or needs help with two or more activities of daily living, it can be more than one person or one family can realistically handle.

If you know what you want, communicate with your family about both the best-case and worst-case scenarios. Then, hope for the best and plan for the worst.

Realistic Cost of Care

Wrapped up in your planning should be a consideration for the cost of long-term care. Although many of us will need some degree of long-term care—including the 30 percent of us who may need up to five years of facility care—60 percent of us underestimate the costs of nursing home care. On average, consumers underestimate the annual cost of a private room in a nursing home by 51 percent.[6]

Another piece of preparing for long-term care costs is anticipating inflation. It's common knowledge that prices have been and keep rising, and that will lower your purchasing power on everything from food to medical care. Long-term care is a big piece of the inflation-disparity pie, which is part of why many find their estimates of nursing home care widely miss the mark. According to one survey, people expected to pay around $25,350 in out-of-pocket long-term care expenses per year, but in reality, they'll more likely pay more than $47,000 annually.[7]

While local costs vary from state to state, here's the annual national median for various forms of long-term care (plus projections that account for 3 percent annual inflation, so you can see what I'm talking about):[8]

---

[6] Tamara E. Holmes. Yahoo Finance. July 24, 2019. "Consumers Underestimate Costs of Long-Term Care."
https://finance.yahoo.com/news/consumers-underestimate-costs-long-term-173542918.html
[7] Moll Law Group. 2019. "The Cost of Long-Term Care."
https://www.molllawgroup.com/the-cost-of-long-term-care.html.
[8] Genworth Financial. June 2018. "Cost of Care Survey 2018."
https://www.genworth.com/aging-and-you/finances/cost-of-care.html.

Long-Term Care Costs: Inflation			
	Home Health Care, Homemaker Services	Adult Day Care	Assisted Living	Nursing Home (semi-private room)
Annual 2018	$48,048	$18,720	$48,000	$89,297
Annual 2028	$64,572	$25,158	$64,508	$120,008
Annual 2038	$86,780	$33,810	$86,693	$161,280
Annual 2048	$116,625	$45,438	$116,509	$216,747

Fund Your Long-Term Care

One big mistake I see are those who haven't planned for long-term care because they assume the government will take care of everything. But that's a huge misconception. The government has two health insurance programs: Medicare and Medicaid. These can greatly assist you in your health care needs in retirement but usually don't provide enough coverage to cover all your health care costs in retirement. My firm isn't a government outpost, so we don't get to make decisions when it comes to forming policy and specifics about either one of these programs. I'm going to give the overview of both, but if you want to get into the details of these programs, you can visit www.Medicare.gov and www.Medicaid.gov.

Medicare

Medicare covers those age sixty-five and older and those who are disabled. Medicare's coverage of any nursing-home-related health issues is limited. It might cover your nursing home stay if it is not a "custodial" stay and it isn't long term. For example, if you break a bone or suffer a stroke and stay in a nursing home for rehabilitative care and then return home, Medicare may cover you. But if you have developed dementia or are looking to move to a nursing facility because you can no longer bathe, dress, toilet, feed yourself, take care of your hygiene, etc., then Medicare is not going to pay for your nursing home costs.[9]

Medicaid

Medicaid is a program that the states administer, so funding, protocol, and limitations vary. Compared to Medicare, Medicaid more widely covers nursing home care, but it targets a different demographic than Medicare: those with low incomes.

If you have more assets than the Medicaid limit in your state and need nursing home care, you will need to use those assets to pay for your care. You will also have a list of additional state-approved ways to spend some of these assets over the Medicaid limit, such as pre-purchasing burial plots and funeral expenses, or paying off debts. After that, your remaining assets fund your nursing home stay until they are gone, at which point Medicaid will jump in.

Some people aren't stymied by this, thinking they will just pass on their financial assets early, gifting them to relatives, friends, and causes so they can qualify for Medicaid when they need it. However, to prevent this exact scenario, Uncle Sam has implemented the look-back period. Currently, if you enroll in Medicaid, you are subject to having the government scrutinize the last five years of your finances for large gifts or expenses that may subject you to penalties, temporarily making you ineligible for Medicaid coverage.

So, if you're planning to preserve your money for future generations and retain control of your financial resources during

---

[9] Medicare.gov. "What Part A covers." https://www.medicare.gov/what-medicare-covers/part-a/what-part-a-covers.html.

your life, you'll probably want to prepare for the costs of longevity beyond a "government plan."

Self-Funding

One way to fund a longer life is the old-fashioned way, through self-funding. There are a variety of financial tools you can use, and they all have their pros and cons. If your assets are in low-interest financial vehicles (savings, bonds, CDs), you risk letting inflation erode the value of your dollar. Or, if you are relying on the stock market, you have more growth potential, but you'll also want to consider the possible implications of market volatility; what if your assets take a hit? If you suffer a loss in your retirement portfolio in early or mid-retirement, you might have the option to "tighten your belt," so to speak, and cut back on discretionary spending to allow your portfolio the room to bounce back. But if you are retired and depend on income from a stock account that just hit a downward stride, what are you going to do?

HSAs

These days, you might also be able to self-fund through a health savings account, or HSA, if you have access to one through a high-deductible health plan (you will not qualify to save in an HSA after enrolling in Medicare). In an HSA, any growth of your tax-deductible contributions will be tax-free, and any distributions that are paid out for qualified health costs are also tax-free. That can be a tax trifecta. Long-term care expenses count as health costs, so, if this is an option available to you, that is one way to use the tax advantages to self-fund your longevity. Bear in mind, if you are younger than sixty-five, any money you use for nonqualified expenses will be subject to taxes and penalties, and, if you are older than sixty-five, any HSA money you use for non-medical expenses is subject to income tax.

LTCI

One slightly more nuanced way to pay for longevity, specifi\u0254ally for long-term care, is long-term care insurance, or LTCI. As car insurance protects your assets in case of a car accident, and home insurance protects your assets in case something happens to your house, long-term care insurance aims to protect your assets in case you need long-term care in an at-home or nursing home situation.

As with other types of insurance, you will pay a monthly or annual premium in exchange for an insurance company paying for long-term care down the road. Typically, policies cover two to three years of care, which is adequate for an "average" situation: it's estimated that 70 percent of Americans will need about three years of long-term care of some kind. However, it's important to consider that you might not be "average" when you are preparing for long-term care costs; on average, 20 percent of today's sixty-five-year-olds could need care for longer than five years.[10]

Now, there are a few oft-cited components of LTCI that make it unattractive for some:

- Expense—LTCI is expensive. It is generally less expensive the younger you are, but a fifty-five-year-old couple who purchased LTCI in 2019 could expect to pay $3,050 each year for an average three-year coverage policy. And the annual cost only increases from there the older you are.[11]
- Limited options—Let's face it: LTCI is often expensive for consumers, but it is also expensive for companies that offer it. With fewer companies willing to take on that

---

[10] David Levine. *U.S. News.* July 10, 2019. "How to Pay for Nursing home Costs." https://health.usnews.com/best-nursing-homes/articles/how-to-pay-for-nursing-home-costs

[11] American Association for Long-Term Care Insurance. January 2019. "2019 National Long-Term Care Insurance Price Index." https://www.aaltci.org/news/wp-content/uploads/2019/01/2019-Price-Index-LTC.pdf

expense, that narrows the market, meaning opportunities to price shop for policies with different options or custom benefits are limited.

- If you know you need it, you might not be able to get it—Insurance companies that offer LTCI are taking on a risk that you may need LTCI. That risk is the foundation of the product—you may or may not need it. If you know you will need it because you have a dementia diagnosis or another illness for which you will need long-term care, you will likely not qualify for LTCI coverage.

- Use it or lose it—If you have LTCI and are in the minority of Americans who die having never needed long-term care, all the money you paid into your LTCI policy is gone.

- Possibly fluctuating rates—Your rate is not locked in on LTCI. Companies maintain the ability to raise or lower your premium amounts. This means some seniors face an ultimatum: Keep funding a policy at what might be a less affordable rate OR lose coverage and let go of all the money they paid in so far.

After that, you might be thinking, "How can people possibly be interested in LTCI?" But let me repeat myself—as many as 70 percent of Americans will need long-term care. And, although only 8 percent of Americans have purchased LTCI, keep in mind the costs of nursing home care. Can you afford $7,000 a month to put into nursing home care and still have enough left over to protect your legacy? This is a very real concern: One study says 72 percent of Americans are impoverished by the end of just one year in a nursing home.[12] So, not to sound like a broken record, but it is vitally important to have a plan in place to deal with longevity and long-term care if you intend to leave a financial legacy.

---

[12] A Place for Mom. January 2018. "Long-Term Care Insurance: Costs & Benefits." http://www.aplaceformom.com/senior-care-resources/articles/long-term-care-costs.

Life Insurance and Annuities

At Sweitzer Income Planning, we have serious long-term care discussions with our clients. We know healthcare costs can erode, and even derail, a retirement income plan if it is not protected.

Our income strategies often include long-term care protections through optional or built-in riders on annuities and life insurance contracts. The recent introduction of these riders created a very substantial change in the world of life insurance. It has allowed our clients to now take a new look at life insurance as a whole. If healthy, clients can review their policies and apply to secure additional health coverage with a chronic illness rider or long-term care rider. These riders are also available on many ten year, twenty year, and thirty year term life insurance policies as well.

Imagine qualifying to receive lump sum payments from your term life insurance while you are alive. Life insurance with these long-term care riders can allow you to cover critical illness and long-term care without losing the premiums you've paid for the policy's primary death benefit if you never need the added coverage. You won't get back any premiums paid for the long term care rider, but your beneficiaries will still receive the policy's death benefit when you die. This is a good example of your one dollar doing many dollars' worth of work.

We offer complimentary life insurance and annuity contract reviews to all our clients as part of our process.

It is not uncommon for us to come across clients who have not efficiently planned for long-term care, either for themselves or for their loved ones. Cari had the heart-wrenching experience of watching a particularly noteworthy story unfold. She had an elderly client who already had a long-term care strategy, complete with a policy providing a pre-set dollar amount to last her three years. Unfortunately, Cari watched the woman's family activate the policy, which paid out for the three specified years. After that, the woman was forced to rely on her other assets as she went on to outlive her long-term care policy by four years.

It was a daily battle between the woman and her insurance provider. Her expenses added up rapidly, and it was a constant struggle to prove qualifying medical expenses. Often, the reimbursement of the money she was eligible for was not given to her. She had a "use-it-or-lose-it" type of policy, which hovered over everyone involved in her care. When she was eligible for the long-term care, there was a rush to start the program because her health was rapidly decreasing. If she had a different policy, then perhaps she would not have needed to deplete all of her other assets in the remaining four years she outlived her coverage.

Spousal Planning

One thing to keep in mind no matter how you plan to save: Many of us will be planning for more than ourselves. Look back at all the stats on health events and the likelihood of long life and long-term care. If they hold true for a single individual, then the likelihood of having a costly health or long-term care event is even higher for a married couple. You'll be planning for not just one life, but two. So, when it comes to long-term care insurance, or annuities, or self-funding, or whatever strategy you are looking at using, be sure you are funding longevity for both of you.

A common saying in our office is "protected money." Protected money is money that isn't subject to the ups and downs of the market. To us, our client's financial longevity is at the core of our business. Financial longevity covers not just the longevity of your own life, but also the life of those you love. Protected money is an important concept to recognize, and, at Sweitzer Income Planning, we also widen our scope to include the financial longevity of everyone in your family.

CHAPTER TWO

Taxes

Where to begin with taxes? Perhaps by acknowledging we all bear responsibility for the resources we share. Roads, bridges, schools . . . It is the patriotic duty of every American to pay his or her fair share of taxes. Many would agree with me, though, that while they don't mind paying their fair share, they're not interested in paying one cent more than that!

Now, just talking taxes probably takes your mind to April, tax season. You are probably thinking about all the forms you collect and how you file. Perhaps you are thinking about your certified public accountant or another qualified tax professional and saying to yourself, "I've already got taxes taken care of, thanks!"

However, what I see when people come into my office is that their relationship with their tax professional is purely a January to April relationship. That means they may have a tax professional, but not a tax *planner*.

What I mean by that is tax planning extends beyond filing taxes. In April, we are required to do an accounting with the IRS to make sure we have paid up on our bill or to settle the score if we have overpaid. But real tax planning is about making each financial move in a way that allows you to keep the most money in your pocket and out of Uncle Sam's.

Now, as a caveat, I want to emphasize that I am not a CPA, nor am I a tax planner, but I see the way taxes affect my clients, and I have plenty of experience helping clients with tax-efficient strategies in their retirement income plans using various insurance and annuity products, in conjunction with their tax professionals.

It is especially important to me to help my clients develop tax-efficient strategies in their retirement income strategies because each dollar they can keep in their pockets is a dollar we can put to work.

We do not offer tax or legal advice at Sweitzer Income Planning, but we work hand in hand with our client's CPAs and attorneys. We find it very important to have the right team of professionals to deliver a tax-efficient income distribution and legacy plan for our clients. Often we prioritize capitalizing on the relationship already established with our client and their personal professionals because we want our clients to feel comfortable and involved in every step of their financial longevity plan.

The Fed

Now, in the United States, taxes can be a rather uncertain proposition. Depending on who is in the White House and which party controls Congress, we might be tempted to assume tax rates could decline or increase in the next four to eight years accordingly. However, there is one (large!) factor that we, as a nation, must confront: the national debt.

Currently, according to USDebtClock.org, we are over $22,000,000,000,000 in debt and climbing. That's $22 TRILLION with a T. With just $1 trillion, you could park it in the bank at a zero percent interest rate and still spend more than $54 million every day for 50 years without hitting a zero balance.

Even if Congress got a handle and stopped that debt from its daily compound, divided by each taxpayer, we each would owe about $175,000. So, will that be check or cash?

My point here isn't to give you anxiety. I'm just saying, even with the rosiest of outlooks on our personal income tax rates, none of us should count on low tax rates for the long term. Instead, you and your network of professionals (tax, legal, and financial) should constantly be looking for ways to take advantage of tax-saving opportunities as they come. After all, the best "luck" is when proper planning meets opportunity.

So, how can we get started?

Know Your Limits

One of the foundational pieces of tax planning is knowing what tax bracket you are in, based on your income after subtracting pre-tax or untaxed assets. Your income taxes are based on your taxable income.

One reason to know your taxable income and your income tax rate is so you can see how far away you are from the next lower or higher tax bracket. This is particularly important when it comes to decisions such as gifting and Roth IRA rollovers. You will want to be sure to talk to a tax professional and a financial advisor registered to provide investment advice before making any decisions.

For instance, based on the 2020 tax table, Mallory and Ralph's taxable income is just over $330,000, putting them in the 32 percent tax bracket and about $3,400 above the upper end of the 24 percent tax bracket. They have already maxed out their retirement funds' tax-exempt contributions for the year. Their daughter, Gloria, is a sophomore in college. This couple can shave more than $2,700 off their tax bill by using that $3,400 to reduce their taxable income by helping Gloria out with groceries and school—something they were likely to do, anyway, but now can deliberately put to work for them in their overall financial strategy.

Now, I use Mallory and Ralph only as an example—your circumstances are probably different—but I think this nicely illustrates the way planning ahead for taxes can save you money.

Assuming a Lower Tax Rate

Many people anticipate being in a lower tax bracket in retirement. It makes sense: You won't be contributing to retirement funds; you'll be drawing from them. And you won't have all those work expenses—work clothes, transportation, etc.

Yet, do you really plan on changing your lifestyle after retirement? Do you plan to cut down on the number of times you eat out, scale back vacations, and skimp on travel?

Taxable Brackets for 2020 Ordinary Income Tax Rates

Marginal Tax Rate	Married Filing Joint	Single
10%	$0-$19,750	$0-$9,875
12%	$19,751-$80,250	$9,876-$40,125
22%	$80,251-$171,050	$40,126-$85,525
24%	$171,051-$326,600	$85,526-$163,300
32%	$326,601-$414,700	$163,301-$207,350
35%	$414,701-$622,050	$207,351-$518,400
37%	$622,051+	$518,401+

What I see in my office is that many couples spend more in the first few years, or maybe the first decade, of retirement. Sure, that may taper off later on, but usually only just in time for their budget to be hit with greater health and long-term care expenses. Do you see where this is going? Many people plan as though their taxable income will be lower in retirement and are surprised when the tax bills come in and look more or less the same as they used to. It's better to plan for the worst and hope for the best, wouldn't you agree?

401(k)/IRA

One sometimes-unexpected piece of tax planning in retirement is in your 401(k) or IRA. Most of us have one of these accounts or an equivalent. Throughout our working lives, we pay in, dutifully socking away a portion of our earnings in these tax-deferred accounts. There's the rub: tax-deferred. Not tax-free. Very rarely is anything free of taxation, when you get down to it. Using 401(k)s and IRAs in retirement is no different. The taxes the government deferred when you were in your working years are now coming due, and you will pay taxes on the earned income from those accounts at whatever your current tax rate is.

Just to ensure Uncle Sam gets his due, the government also has a required minimum distribution, or RMD, rule. Beginning at age seventy 72, you are required to withdraw a certain minimum amount every year from your 401(k) or IRA, or you will face a 50 percent tax penalty on any RMD monies you should have withdrawn but didn't, and that's on top of income tax.

Of course, there is also the Roth account. You can think of the difference between a Roth and a traditional retirement account as the difference between taxing the seed and taxing the harvest. Because Roths are funded with post-tax dollars, there aren't tax penalties for early withdrawals of the principal, nor are there taxes on the growth after you reach age fifty-nine-and-one-half. Perhaps best of all, there are no RMDs. Of course, you must own a Roth account for a minimum of five years before you are able to take advantage of all its features.

This is one more area where it pays to be aware of your tax bracket. Some people may find it advantageous to "convert" their traditional retirement account funds to Roth account funds in a year during which they are in a lower tax bracket. Others may opt to put any excess RMDs from their traditional retirement accounts into other products, like stocks or insurance.

Does that make your head spin? Understandable. That's why it's so important to work with a financial professional and tax planner who can help you not only execute these sorts of tax-

strategies but also help you understand what you are
ˌg and why.

We have only two certainties to rely on in life: we will be taxed, and we will die. The income tax brackets are lower, as of the writing of this book, than they have been in a long time. However, our deficit is growing, resulting in the lack of sufficient funding for Social Security and Medicare in the long run. As a result, we must recognize a few tax-efficient planning opportunities today. In our current climate, a Roth IRA conversion provides a great tax planning tool.

A client of mine strongly felt tax rates would be higher during his peak retirement years. As a result, this client converted $100,000 of his IRA to a Roth IRA, resulting in a 24 percent tax bracket. The $24,000 check for taxes was a hard check to write. However, it made good financial sense for him to pay 24 percent in taxes now and never pay taxes again on the $100,000. The $100,000 Roth can now grow tax-deferred, he can withdraw his income tax-free, and he can also leave the Roth to his spouse or kids completely tax-free.

Conventional wisdom tells us to defer taxes as long as possible. That is effective tax planning, if the tax rates either stay the same or lower in the future. With the sunset of the 2017 Tax Cuts and Jobs Act scheduled for 2026, unless Congress initiates a new tax bill, taxes will *not* stay the same or lower in the future. Instead, they will rise back to their pre-2018 rates. Thus, it seems wise to pay taxes now rather than putting them off. For example, in a 50 percent tax bracket, a client would have to withdraw $100,000 from his IRA to net $50,000—historical marginal tax rates have been higher than 90 percent at times. Yet, this client payed only 24 percent today to never pay taxes on that money again.

Tax-deferred is great, but, in many situations, tax-free is even better. This client converted "later tax dollars" into "never-again-taxed dollars."

CHAPTER THREE

Market Volatility

"Everything not saved will be lost."
-Nintendo "Quit Screen" message

U p and down. Roller coaster. Merry-go-round. Bulls and bears. Peak-to-trough.

Sound familiar? This is the language we use to talk about the stock market. With volatility and spikes, even our language is jarring, bracing, vivid.

Still, financial strategies tend to revolve around market-based products because there is no other financial class that packs the same potential for growth, pound for pound, as stock-based products.

However, along with the potential for growth is the potential for loss. Many of the people I see in my office come in still feeling a bit burned from the market drama of 2000 to 2010. That was a rough stretch.

So how do we balance these factors? How do we try to satisfy both the need for protection and the need for growth?

For one thing, it is important to recognize the value of diversity. Now, I'm not just talking about the diversity of assets among different kinds of stocks, or even different kinds of stocks and bonds. That's only one kind of diversity; both stocks and bonds, while different, are still market-based products. Most rket-based products tend to rise or lower as a whole, just like an incoming tide. Therefore, a diverse portfolio won't automatically protect your assets during times when the market is declining.

In addition to the sort of "horizontal diversity" you have by purchasing a variety of stocks and bonds from different companies, I encourage having "vertical diversity," or diversity among asset classes. This means having different product types, with varying levels of growth potential, liquidity, and protection, all in accordance with your unique situation, goals, and needs. This will often involve the assistance of a securities-registered individual who can offer you investment products for your portfolio, when needed.

The Rule of 100 is a widely used rule of thumb to determine what percentage of one's portfolio should be protected from market loss. In theory, you take your age and subtract it from 100. The resulting number designates the percentage of your portfolio that could be at risk. For example, a client is sixty years old. According to the Rule of 100, this client should have no more than 40 percent of their assets at risk in the stock market, and 60 percent of the assets should be invested in principal-protected growth assets. At Sweitzer Income Planning, the Rule of 100 simply provides a starting point to communicate about risk with our clients. Using the input and feedback from clients, we help them determine their own suitable asset allocation.

The Color of Money

When you're looking at the overall diversity of your portfolio, part of the equation is knowing which products fit in what category: what has liquidity, what has protection, and what has growth potential.

Before we dive into that, keep in mind that these aren't absolutes. You might think of liquidity, growth, and protection as primary colors. While some products will look pretty much yellow, red, or blue, others will have a mix of characteristics, making them more green, orange, or purple.

Growth

I like to think of the growth category as red. It's powerful, it's somewhat volatile, and it's also the category where we have the biggest opportunities for growth and loss. Sometimes products in the growth category have a good deal of liquidity but very little protection. These are our market-based products and strategies, so we're thinking mostly shades of red and orange. This is a good place to be when you're young—think fast cars and flashy leather jackets—but its allure often wanes as you get closer to retirement. Examples of "red" products include:

- Stocks
- Equities
- Exchange-traded funds
- Mutual funds
- Corporate bonds
- Real estate investment trusts
- Speculations
- Alternative investments

Liquidity

Yellow is my liquid category color. I typically recommend having at least enough yellow money to cover six months to a year's worth of expenses in case of emergency. Yellow assets don't need a lot of growth potential; they just need to be readily available when we need them. The "yellow" category includes:

- Cash
- Money market accounts

Protection

The color of protection, to me, is blue. Tranquil, peaceful, sure, even if it lacks a certain amount of flash. This is the direction I like to see people generally move toward as they're nearing retirement. The red, flashy look of stock market returns and the risk of possible overnight losses is less attractive as we near retirement and look for more consistency and reliability. While this category doesn't come with a lot of liquidity, the products here are backed by an insurance company, a bank, or a government entity. "Blue" products include:

- Certificates of deposit (backed by the bank)
- Government-based bonds (backed by the government)
- Life insurance (backed by the companies)
- Annuities (backed by the companies)

Dollar-Cost Averaging

With 401(k)s and other market-based retirement products (IRAs, 403(b)s, etc.), when you are investing for the long term, dollar-cost averaging is a concept that can work in your favor. When the market is trending up, if you are consistently paying in money, month over month, great; your investments are growing, and you are adding to your assets. When the market takes a dip, no problem; your dollars buy more shares at a lower price. At some point, we hope the market will rebound, in which case your shares will fatten up and possibly be more valuable than they were before. This phenomenon is what we call dollar-cost averaging. While it can't ensure a profit or guarantee against losses, it's a time-tested strategy for investing in a volatile market.

However, when you are in retirement, this may work against you. You may even hear of "reverse" dollar-cost averaging. Before, when the market lost ground, you were bargain-shopping; your dollars purchased more assets at a reduced price. When you are in retirement, you are no longer the purchaser; you are selling. So in a down market, you have to sell more assets to make the same amount of money as you did in a positive market.

I've had lots of people step into my office saying, "My advisor says the market always bounces back and that I have to just hold on for the long term."

There's a basis for this thinking; thus far, the market has always rebounded, often to even higher heights than before. But this is no guarantee, and the prospect of potentially higher returns in five years may not be very helpful in retirement if you are relying on the income from those returns to pay this month's electric bill, for example. That's why at our firm, we specialize in insurance strategies that help provide a reliable stream of income.

Life insurance companies offer a product called a fixed index annuity that provides guaranteed lifetime income for many of our clients. Similar to the income stream from a pension or Social Security, the income will be paid every month as long as you live. While this account is paying you income (assuming you don't take income by annuitization), you get to control the remainder of your principal. Many annuities also offer an enhanced death benefit feature and optional protection for long term healthcare costs. These annuities provide a good fit for many of our clients who don't want to take risk with their income from investing it in the stock market and who want the potential for competitive interest growth, too.

Is There a "Perfect" Product?

To bring us back around to the discussion of protection, growth, and liquidity, the ideal product would be a "ten" in all three categories, right? Completely guaranteed, doubling in size every few years, and accessible whenever you want. Does such a product exist? Anyone who says yes is either ignorant or malevolent.

Instead of running in circles looking for that perfect product, the silver bullet, the unicorn of financial strategies, it's more important to circle back to the concept of a balanced, asset-diverse retirement portfolio.

This is why your interests may be best served when you work with a team of qualified financial professionals who know what various financial products can do and how to use them in your personal retirement plan.

Unfortunately, there is no way to avoid inflation. However, some financial vehicles, such as a fixed index annuity, offer the potential for conservative growth to help consumers address and manage inflation over the long term. The issuing company locks in your principal and the growth of the fixed index annuity each year, and you are not at risk for loss due to market volatility.

CHAPTER FOUR

Retirement Income

Retirement. For many of us, it's what we've saved for and dreamed of, pinning our hopes to a magical someday. Is that someday filled with traveling? Spoiling the grandkids? Gardening? Maybe your fondest dream is simply never having to work again, never having to clock in or be accountable to someone else.

Your ability to do these things all hinges on INCOME. Without the money to support these dreams, even a basic level of work-free lifestyle is unsustainable. That's why planning for your income in retirement is so crucially foundational. But where to begin?

It's easy to be overwhelmed by this question. Some may feel the urge to amass a large lump sum and then try to put it all in one product—insurance, investments, liquid assets—to provide all the growth, liquidity, and income they need. I think you need a more balanced approach. After all, retirement planning isn't magic. There is no single product that can be all things to all people, or even all things to one person. No approach works unilaterally for everyone. That's why it's important to talk to a financial professional who can help you lay down the basics and take you step-by-step through the process. Not only will you have the assurance that you have addressed the areas you need to, but you will also have an ally who can help you break it down and help keep you from feeling overwhelmed.

Sources of Income

Thinking of all the pieces of your retirement expenses might be intimidating. But, like cleaning out a junk drawer or revisiting that garage remodel, once you have laid everything out, you can begin to sort things into categories.

Once you have a good overall picture of where your expenses will lie, you can start stacking up the resources to cover them.

Social Security

Social Security is a guaranteed, inflation-protected federal insurance program that plays a big part in most of our retirement plans. From delaying until you've reached full retirement age or beyond to examining spousal benefits, as I discuss elsewhere in this book, there is plenty you can do to try to make the most of this monthly benefit. As with all your retirement income sources, it's important to consider how to make this resource stretch to give you the most bang and buck for your situation.

Pension

Another generally reliable source of retirement income for you might be a pension, if you are one of the lucky people who still has one.

If you don't have a pension, go ahead and skim on to the next section. If you do have a pension, keep on reading.

Because your pension can be such a central piece of your retirement income plan, you will want to put some thought into answering basic questions about it.

How well is your pension funded? Since the heyday of the pension plan, companies and governments neglecting to fund their pension obligations has been a persistent problem with this otherwise reliable asset. A report by the American Legislative Exchange Council revealed there was a $5.96 trillion deficit in state pension funds overall in 2018.[13] If you have a pension, it is quite possibly included in that statistic.

In addition to checking up on your pension's health, check into what your options are for withdrawing your pension. If you have already retired and made those decisions, this may be a foregone conclusion. If not, though, it pays to know what you can expect and what decisions you can make, such as taking spousal options that will cover your husband or wife if he or she outlives you.

Also, some companies are incentivizing lump-sum payouts of pensions to reduce the companies' payment liabilities. If that's the case with your employer, talk to your financial professional to see if it might be prudent to do something like that or if it might be better to stick with lifetime payments or other options.

Your 401(k) and IRA

One "modern way" to save for retirement is in a 401(k) or IRA (or their nonprofit or governmental equivalents). These tax-advantaged accounts are, in my opinion, a poor substitute for pensions. However, one of the biggest disservices we do to ourselves in our working years is to not take full advantage of them in the first place. According to one article, about 42 percent of adults under thirty and 26 percent of adults thirty to forty-four haven't contributed to any retirement account, let alone their 401(k).[14]

Also, if you have changed jobs over the years, do the work of tracking down any benefits from your past employers. You might have an IRA here or a 401(k) there; keep track of those so

---

[13] Jonathan Williams, Christine Smith, Thurston Powers, and Bob Williams. ALEC. "Unaccountable and Unaffordable 2018." https://www.alec.org/publication/unaccountable-and-unaffordable-2018/March 20, 2019.

[14] Niall McCarthy. Forbes. June 3, 2019. "Report: A Quarter of Americans Have No Retirement Savings." https://www.forbes.com/sites/niallmccarthy/2019/06/03/report-a-quarter-of-americans-have-no-retirement-savings-infographic/#5fb35b703ebf

you can pull them together and look at those assets when you're ready to look at establishing sources of retirement income.

Do You Have…
- Life insurance?
- Annuities?
- Long-term care insurance?
- Any passive income sources?
- Stock and bond portfolios?
- Liquid assets? What's in your bank account?
- Alternative investments?
- Rental properties?

It's important, if you are going through the work of sitting with a financial professional, to look at your full retirement income picture and pull together ALL your assets, no matter how big or small. From the free insurance policy offered at your bank to the sizable investment in your brother-in-law's modestly successful furniture store, you want to have a good idea of where your money is.

Some people feel planning for retirement is for when you are in your fifties. It is not. When Cari and I got married thirty years ago, we both purchased life insurance. Cari had a small life insurance policy at work with United Airlines and felt as if she did not need any additional coverage. I told her when she eventually stopped working for United, she would lose the life insurance. We didn't know when she would leave United or what her health situation would be at that time. So, she decided to acquire a new life insurance policy, as well.

A few months later, Cari's college roommate got married to a fellow USC graduate. Cari emphasized the importance of life insurance to her during this time of change. Thanks, in part, to Cari's encouragement, both her friend and her husband took out life insurance policies. Ten years later, her husband committed suicide, leaving her behind with two beautiful children. It wasn't until then that she recognized and appreciated the insurance policy she took out ten years prior. With all the grief of her loss and the fear of the unknown, she was grateful they acted so shrewdly long before. The life insurance aided her in the years to come with expenses, mortgages, college tuitions, and even some for her eventual retirement.

In the long run, life insurance is not about you, it is about the people you leave behind. This sad illustration identifies the importance of planning for the unexpected.

Retirement Income Needs

How much income will you need in retirement? How do you determine that? A lot of people work toward a random number, thinking, "If I can just have a million dollars, I'll be comfortable in retirement!" Don't get me wrong; it is possible to save up a lot of money and then retire in the hopes that you can keep your monthly expenses lower than some set estimation. But I think this carries a risk of running out of money. Instead, I work with my clients to find out what their current and projected income needs are and then work from there to see how we might cover any gaps between what they have and what they want.

Goals and Dreams

I like to start with your pie in the sky. Do you find yourself planning for your vacations more thoroughly than you do your retirement? Maybe it's because planning a vacation is less stressful: Having a week at the beach go awry is, well, a walk on the beach compared to running out of money in retirement. Whatever the case, perhaps it would be better if you think of your retirement as a vacation in and of itself—no clocking in, no boss, no overtime. If you felt unlimited by financial strain, what would you do?

Would an endless vacation for you mean Paris and Rome? Would it mean mentoring at children's clubs or serving at the local soup kitchen? Or maybe it would mean deepening your ties to those immediately around you—neighbors, friends, and family. Maybe it would mean more time to take part in hobbies and activities you love. Have you been considering a second (or even third) act as a small-business owner, turning a hobby or passion into a revenue source?

This is your time to daydream and answer the question: If you could do anything, what would you do?

After that, it's a matter of putting a dollar amount on it. What are the costs of round-the-world travel? One couple I know said their biggest priority in retirement was being able to take each of their grandchildren on a cross-country vacation every year. That's a pretty specific goal—and one that is reasonably easy to nail down a budget for.

Current Budget

Compiling a current expense report can be one of the trickiest pieces of retirement preparation. Many people assume the expenses of their lives in retirement will be different, lower. After all, there will be no drive to work, no need to keep a formal wardrobe, and, perhaps most impactful of all, no more saving for retirement!

Yet, we often underestimate our daily spending habits. That's why I typically ask my clients to bring in their bank statements for the past year—they are reflective of your ACTUAL spending, not just what you think you're spending.

I can't count the number of times I have sat with a couple, asked them about their spending, and heard them give me a number that seems incredibly low. When I ask them where it came from, they usually have estimated based on their total bills. Yet, our spending is so much more than our mortgage, utilities, cable, phone, car, grocery, or credit card bills.

"What about clothes?" I ask. "Or dining out? What about gifts and coffees and last-minute birthday cards?" That's when the lights come on.

This is why I suggest collecting a year's worth of information. There is usually no such thing as a one-time purchase. Did you buy new furniture? Even if that is a rarity, do you think that will be the last time you EVER buy furniture?

Another big one is spending on the kids. Many of the couples I work with are quick to help their adult children, whether it's something like letting them live in the basement, paying for college, babysitting, paying an occasional bill, or contributing to a grandchild's college fund. They aren't alone—79 percent of Americans in 2018 said they had provided financial support for an adult child. And it's not unlikely for some parents to tap into their retirement funds to do so.[15]

My clients sometimes protest that what they do for their grown children can stop in retirement. They don't NEED to help. But I get it. Parents like to feel needed. And, while you never want to neglect saving for retirement in favor of taking on financial risks like your child's student debt, the parents who help their adult children do so in part because it helps them feel fulfilled.

When it comes down to expenses, including, and especially, spending on your family, don't make your initial calculations based on what you COULD whittle your budget down to if you HAD to. Instead, start from where you are. Who wants to live off a bare-bones bank account in retirement?

Other Expenses

Once you have nailed down your current budget and your dreams or goals for retirement, there are a few other outstanding pieces to think about—some expenses that many people don't take the time to consider before making and executing a plan. But I assume you want to get it right, so let's take a look.

---

[15] Lorie Konish. CNBC. October 2, 2018. "Parents Spend Twice as Much on Adult Children than They Save for Retirement." https://www.cnbc.com/2018/10/02/parents-spend-twice-as-much-on-adult-children-than-saving-for-retirement.html.

Housing

Do you know where you want to live in retirement? This is a big piece of your income puzzle—since the typical American household owns a home, and it's generally their largest asset[16]—but one that often goes unaccounted for until the last minute.

Some people prefer to live right where they are for as long as they can. Others have been waiting for retirement to pull the trigger on an ambitious move, like purchasing a new house, or even downsizing. Whatever your plans and whatever your reasons, there are quite a few things to consider.

Mortgage

Do you still have a mortgage? What may have been a nice tax boon in your working years could turn into a financial burden in your retirement. After all, when you are on a limited income, a mortgage is just one more bill sapping your financial strength. It is something to put some thought into, whether you plan to age in place or are considering moving to your dream home, buying a house out of state, or living in a retirement community.

Upkeep and Taxes

A house without a mortgage still requires annual taxes. While it's tempting to think of this as a once-a-year expense, when you have limited earning potential, your annual tax bill might be something into which you should put a little more forethought.

The costs of homeownership aren't just monetary. When you find yourself dealing with more house than you need, it can drain your time and energy. From keeping clutter at bay to keeping the lawn mower running, upkeep can be extensive and expensive. For some, that's a challenge they heartily accept and can comfortably take on. For others, the idea of yard work or cleaning an area larger than they need feels foolish.

---

[16] Jann Swanson. Mortgage News Daily. August 28, 2019. "Homeownership is the Top Contributor to Household Wealth." http://www.mortgagenewsdaily.com/08282019_homeownership.asp

For instance, Peggy discovered after her knee replacement that most of her house was inaccessible to her when she was laid up.

"It felt ridiculous to pay someone else to dust and vacuum a house I was only living in 40 percent of!"

Practicality and Adaptability

Erik and Magda are looking to retire within the next two decades. They just sold their old three-bedroom ranch-style house. Their twins are in high school, and the couple had wanted to "upgrade" for years. Now they live in a gorgeous 1940s three-story house with all the kitchen space they ever wanted, five sprawling bedrooms, and a library and media room for themselves and their children. Within months of moving in, the couple realized that a house perfect for their active teens would no longer be perfect in five to fifteen years.

"We are already paying the mortgage for this house, but we've started saving for the next one," said Magda, "because who wants to be going up two flights of stairs to their bedroom when they're seventy-eight?"

Others I know have encountered similar situations in their personal lives. After a health crisis, one couple found the luxurious tub for two they toiled to install had become a specter of a bad slip and a potential safety risk. It's important to think through what your physical reality could be, whatever your long-term plan might be; it's amazing how many people don't.

Contracts and Regulations

If you are looking into a cross-country move, be aware of new tax tables or local ordinances in the area where you are looking to move. After all, you don't want to experience sticker-shock when you are looking at downsizing or reducing your bills in retirement.

Along the same lines, if you are moving into a retirement community, be sure to look at the fine print. What will happen if you must move into a different situation for long-term care? Will you be penalized? Will you be responsible for replacing your slot in the community? What are all the fees, and what do they cover?

Inflation

As I write this in 2020, America has experienced a long stretch of low inflation, with average annual inflation not exceeding 4 percent since 1991.[17]

However, inflation isn't a one-time bump; it has a cumulative effect. Even with relatively low inflation over the past few decades, the $20 sneakers you bought your grade-schooler in 1991 will cost $37.33 to buy for your grandchild today.[18] What if, in retirement, we hit a stretch like the late '70s and early '80s, when annual inflation rates of 10 percent became the norm? It may be wise to consider some extra padding in your retirement income plan to account for any potential increase in inflation in the future.

Aging

Also in the expense category, think about longevity. We all hope to age gracefully. However, it's important to face the prospect of aging with a sense of realism.

The elephant in the room for many families is long-term care: No one wants to admit they will likely need it, but it's estimated that as many as 70 percent of us will.[19] Aging is a significant piece of retirement income planning because you'll want to figure out how to set aside money for your care, either at home or away from it. The more comfortable you get with discussing your wishes and plans with your loved ones, the easier planning for the financial side of it can be.

---

[17] US Inflation Calculator. January 2020. "Historical Inflation Rates." http://www.usinflationcalculator.com/inflation/historical-inflation-rates/.
[18] Ibid.
[19] Moll Law Group. 2019. "The Cost of Long-Term Care." https://www.molllawgroup.com/the-cost-of-long-term-care.html.

I discuss health care and potential long-term care costs in more detail elsewhere in this book, but, suffice it to say that nursing home care is incredibly expensive and typically isn't something you get to choose when you need.

It isn't just the costs of long-term care that pose a concern in living longer. It's also about covering the possible costs of everything else associated with living longer. For instance, if Henry retires from his job as a biochemical engineer at age sixty-five, perhaps he planned to have a very decent income for twenty years, until age eighty-five. But what if he lives until he's ninety-five? That's a whole third more—ten years—of personal income he will need.

Putting It All Together

Whew! So you have pulled together what you have, and you have a pretty good idea of where you want to be. Now your financial professional and you can go about the work of arranging what you *have* to cover what you *need*—and how you might try to cover any gaps.

Like the proverbial man in the Bible who built his house on a rock, I like to help my clients figure out how to cover their day-to-day living expenses—their needs—with insurance and other guaranteed income sources like pensions and Social Security.

Sweitzer Income Planning understands no two people are the same, and, thus, no two approaches should be identical. We tailor each financial longevity strategy to a specific person, seeking to provide each client with the necessary income to live on and to last a lifetime. Cari and I do not charge planning fees; rather, we receive direct compensation through commissions from the many insurance companies who provide guarantees and contracts for our clients. The only cost to you for a visit and a general strategy session is your time. When you meet with us, we take our time to evaluate your needs and how you picture your future retirement. We will listen to your worries and concerns to form a complete understanding of how to best evaluate and build strategies designed to deliver the income you need to reach financial longevity.

Again, you should keep in mind that there isn't one single financial vehicle, asset, or source that can fill all your needs, and that's okay. One of the challenges of planning for your income in retirement is figuring out what products and strategies to use. You can let go of some of that stress when you accept that you will need a diverse portfolio, not just one massive money pile.

One way to help shore up your income gaps is by working with your financial professional and a qualified tax advisor to mitigate your tax exposure. Effective tax planning isn't necessarily about "adding" to your income; especially with retirement, it's less about what you make than it is about what you keep. Paying a lower tax bill keeps more money in your pocket, which is where you want it when it comes to retirement income.

Now you can look at ways to cover your remaining retirement goals. Are there products like long-term care insurance that are specific to a certain kind of expense you anticipate? Is there a particular asset you want to use for your "play" money—that money for trips and gifting for the grandkids? Is there any way you can portion off money for those charitable legacy plans?

Once you have analyzed your income wants and needs and the assets to realistically cover them, you may have a gap. The masterstroke of a competent financial professional will be to help you figure out how you will cover that gap. Will you perhaps need to cut out a round of golf a week? Maybe skip the new car? Or will you need to take more significant action?

One way to cover an income gap is to consider working longer before retirement or working part time even after that magical calendar date. This may not be the best "plan" for you; disabilities, work demands, and physical or emotional limitations can stymie the best-laid plans to continue working. However, if it is physically possible for you, this is one big way to help your assets last, for more than one reason.

In fact, about one in five Americans are still working past age sixty-five. This is a record percentage in the past half-century.

While some do list their personal finances as a reason for staying on the job, others do so to avoid feeling bored in retirement, among other reasons.[20]

I had a client come into my office asking when he could retire. This client wanted to start planning to travel the country with his wife for the next chapter of his life. As I reviewed their financials, it appeared that they had enough principal-protected monthly income to retire right away. They were so excited to hop into their RV to start their adventures. A year later, I reached out to schedule their annual review. The client informed me he had just been diagnosed with pancreatic cancer. Having had my mother die of pancreatic cancer ten years prior, I was all too familiar with what follows a diagnosis. It was only six weeks from diagnosis to death for my mother, and this unfortunate man had a similarly short timeline. After his funeral, I spoke to his wife. She was so thankful they at least had that one year in their RV making memories she will always cherish. Not everyone needs to hop in their RV and travel the country. Most of our clients simply want the ability to spend with confidence and live a stress-free retirement. Either way, it is my job to help them discover their own retirement timeline.

When you're retired, you no longer have an employer paying you a steady check. It is up to you to make sure you have saved and planned for the income you need.

---

[20] Associated Press. October 9, 2018. "1 in 5 Americans over 65 are Still Waiting to Retire." https://nypost.com/2018/10/09/1-in-5-americans-over-65-are-still-waiting-to-retire/

CHAPTER FIVE

Social Security

S ocial Security is often the foundation of retirement income. Backed by the strength of the U.S. Treasury, it provides perhaps the most dependable paycheck you will have in retirement.

From the time you collect your first paycheck from the job that made you a bona fide taxpayer (for Cari, it was as a flight attendant for United Airlines), you are paying into the grand old Social Security system. What grew and developed out of the pressures of the Great Depression has become one of the most popular government programs in the country, and if you pay in for the equivalent of ten years or more, you, too, can benefit from the Social Security program.

Now, before we get into the nitty-gritty of Social Security, I'd like to address a current concern: Will Social Security still be there for you when you reach retirement age?

The Future of Social Security

This question is ever-present as headlines trumpet an underfunded Social Security program, alongside the sea of baby boomers who are retiring in droves and the comparatively smaller pool of younger people who are bearing the responsibility of funding the system.

The Social Security Administration itself acknowledges this concern as each Social Security statement now bears an asterisk that continues near the end of the summary:

41

"*Your estimated benefits are based on current law. Congress has made changes to the law in the past and can do so at any time. The law governing benefit amounts may change because, by 2034, the payroll taxes collected will be enough to pay only about 79 percent of scheduled benefits."

Just a reminder, as if you needed one, that nothing in life is guaranteed.

Before you get too discouraged, though, here are a few thoughts to keep you going:

- Although those who retire after 2034 may only receive 79 cents on the dollar for their scheduled benefits, 79 percent is notably not zero.
- The Social Security Administration has made changes in the distant and near past to protect the fund's solvency, including increasing retirement ages and striking certain filing strategies.
- There are many changes that Congress could make and that lawmakers are currently discussing to fix the system, such as further increasing full retirement age and eligibility.
- One thing that no one is seriously discussing. Reneging on current obligations to retirees or the soon-to-retire.

Take heart. The real answer to the question, "Will Social Security be there for me?" is still yes.

This question is an important one to consider when you look at how much we, as a nation, rely on this program. Did you know Social Security benefits replace about 40 percent of a person's original income when they retire? [21]

---

[21] Social Security Administration. "Learn About Social Security Programs." https://www.ssa.gov/planners/retire/r&m6.html.

If you ask me, that's a pretty significant piece of your retirement income puzzle.

Another caveat? You may not realize this, but no one can legally "advise" you about your Social Security benefits.

"But, Ken," you may be thinking, "isn't that part of what you do? And what about that nice gentleman at the Social Security Administration office I spoke with on the phone?"

Don't get me wrong. Social Security Administration employees know their stuff. They are trained to know the policies, and they are usually pretty quick to tell you what you can and cannot do. But the government specifically says that, because Social Security is a benefit that you alone have paid into and earned, your Social Security decisions, too, are yours alone.

When it comes to financial professionals, we can't push you in any directions, either, BUT—there's a big but, here—working with a well-informed financial professional is still incredibly handy when it comes to your Social Security decisions. Why? Because someone who's worth his or her salt will know what withdrawal strategies might pertain to your specific situation and will ask questions that can help you determine what you are looking for when it comes to your Social Security.

For instance, some people want the highest possible monthly benefit. Others want to start their benefits early—and not always because of financial need. I heard of one man who called in to start his Social Security payments the day he qualified, just because he liked to think of it as the government paying back a debt it owed him and enjoyed the feeling of receiving a check from Uncle Sam.

Whatever your reasons, questions, or feelings regarding Social Security, the decision is yours alone, but working with a financial professional can help you put your options in perspective by showing you—both with industry knowledge and with proprietary software or planning processes—where your benefits fit into your overall strategy for retirement income.

One reason the federal government doesn't allow for "advice" related to Social Security, I suspect, is so no one can profit from giving you advice related to your Social Security benefit—or from providing any clarifications. Again, this is a sign of a good financial professional. Those who are passionate about their work will be knowledgeable about what benefit strategies might be to your advantage and will happily share those possible options with you.

Full Retirement Age

When it comes to Social Security, it seems like many people only think so far as "yes." They don't take the time to understand the various options. Instead, because it is common knowledge you can begin your benefits at age sixty-two, that's what many of us do. While more people are opting to delay taking benefits, age sixty-two is still firmly the most popular age to start.[22]

What many people fail to understand is that, by starting benefits early, they may be leaving a lot of money on the table. You see, the Social Security Administration bases your monthly benefit on two factors: your earnings history and your full retirement age (FRA).

From your earnings history, they pull the thirty-five years you made the most money and use a mathematical indexing formula to figure out a monthly average from those years. If you paid into the system for less than thirty-five years, then every year you didn't pay in will be counted as a zero.

Once they have calculated what your monthly earning would be at FRA, the government then calculates what to put on your check based on how close you are to FRA. FRA was originally set at sixty-five, but, as the population aged and lifespans lengthened, the government shifted FRA later and later, based on an individual's year of birth. Check out the following chart to see when you will reach FRA.[23]

---

[22] Elizabeth O'Brien. Money. March 7, 2019. "This is the Age when Most People Claim Social Security—and When Experts Say You Really Should." http://money.com/money/5637694/this-is-the-age-when-most-people-claim-social-security-and-when-experts-say-you-really-should/.
[23] Social Security Administration. "Full Retirement Age." https://www.ssa.gov/planners/retire/retirechart.html.

Age to Receive Full Social Security Benefits*	
(Called "full retirement age" [FRA] or "normal retirement age.")	
Year of Birth*	FRA
1937 or earlier	65
1938	65 and 2 months
1939	65 and 4 months
1940	65 and 6 months
1941	65 and 8 months
1942	65 and 10 months
1943-1954	66
1955	66 and 2 months
1956	66 and 4 months
1957	66 and 6 months
1958	66 and 8 months
1959	66 and 10 months
1960 and later	67

*If you were born on Jan. 1 of any year, you should refer to the previous year. (If you were born on the 1st of the month, we figure your benefit (and your full retirement age) as if your birthday was in the previous month.)

When you reach FRA, you are eligible to receive 100 percent of whatever the Social Security Administration says is your full monthly benefit.

Starting at age sixty-two, for every year before FRA you claim benefits, your monthly check is reduced by 5 percent or more. Conversely, for every year you delay taking benefits past FRA, your monthly benefit increases by 8 percent (until age seventy—after that, there is no monetary advantage to delaying Social Security benefits). While your circumstances and needs may vary, a lot of financial professionals still urge people to at least consider delaying until age seventy.

Why Wait?[24]

Taking benefits early could affect your monthly check by ___.								
62	63	64	65	FRA 66	67	68	69	70
-25 %	-20 %	-13.3 %	-6.7 %	0	+8 %	+16 %	+24 %	+32 %

My Social Security

If you are over age thirty, you have probably received a notice from the Social Security Administration telling you to activate something called My Social Security. This is a handy way to learn more about your particular benefit options and to keep track of what your earnings record looks like and the benefits you have accrued over the years.

Essentially, My Social Security is an online account that you can activate to see what your personal Social Security picture looks like, which you can do at www.ssa.gov/myaccount. This can be extremely helpful when it comes to planning for income

---

[24] Social Security Administration. April 2019. "Can You Take Your Benefits Before Full Retirement Age?" https://www.ssa.gov/planners/retire/applying2.html.

in retirement and figuring up the difference between your anticipated income versus anticipated expenses.

My Social Security is also helpful because it's a great way to see if there is a problem. For instance, I have heard of one woman who, through diligently checking her tax records against her Social Security profile, discovered her Social Security check was shortchanging her, based on her earnings history. After taking the discrepancy to the Social Security Administration, they sent her what they owed her in makeup benefits.

COLA

Social Security is a largely guaranteed piece of the retirement puzzle: If you get a statement that says to expect $1,000 a month, you can be sure that you will get $1,000 a month. But there is one detail that is variable, and that is something called the cost-of-living adjustment, or COLA.

The COLA is an increase in your monthly check that is meant to address inflation in everyday life. After all, your expenses will likely continue to experience inflation in retirement, but you will no longer have the opportunity for raises, bonuses, or promotions that you had when you were working. Instead, Social Security receives an annual cost-of-living increase tied to the Department of Labor's Consumer Price Index for Urban Wage Earners and Clerical Workers, or CPI-W. If the CPI-W measurement shows inflation rose a certain amount for regular goods and services, then Social Security recipients will see that reflected in their COLA.

The COLA averages 4 percent, but in a no- or low-inflation environment, such as in 2010, 2011 and 2016, Social Security recipients will not get an adjustment. Some see the COLA as a perk, bump, or bonus, but in reality, it works more like this: Your mom sends you to the store with $2.50 for a gallon of milk. Milk costs exactly $2.50. The next week, you go back with that same amount, but it is now $2.52 for a gallon, so you go back to Mom, and she gives you 2 cents. You aren't bringing home more milk—it just costs more money.

So the COLA is less about "making more money" and more about keeping seniors' purchasing power from eroding when inflation is a big factor, such as in 1975, when it was 8 percent![25] Still, don't let that detract from your enthusiasm about COLAs; after all, what if Mom's solution was: "Here's the same $2.50; try to find pennies from somewhere else to get that milk!"?

Spousal Benefits

We've talked about FRA, but another big Social Security decision involves spousal benefits.

If you or your spouse has a long stretch of zeros in your earnings history—perhaps one of you stayed home for years, caring for children or sick relatives—you may want to consider filing for spousal benefits instead of filing on your own earnings history. A spousal benefit can be up to 50 percent of the primary wage earner's benefit at full retirement age.

To begin drawing a spousal benefit, you must be at least sixty-two years old, and the primary wage earner must have already filed for his or her benefit. While there are penalties for taking spousal benefits early (you could lose up to 67.5 percent of your check for filing at age sixty-two), you cannot earn credits for delaying.[26]

Like I said, the spousal benefit can be a big deal for those who don't have a very long pay history, but it's important to weigh your own earned benefits against the option of withdrawing based on a fraction of your spouse's benefits.

To look at how this could play out, let's use a hypothetical example of Mary Jane, who is sixty, and Peter, who is sixty-two.

Let's say that Peter's benefit at FRA, in his case sixty-six, would be $1,600. If Peter begins his benefits right now, four years before FRA, his monthly check will be $1,200. If Mary Jane begins taking spousal benefits in two years, at the earliest

---

[25] Social Security Administration. "Cost-Of-Living Adjustment (COLA) Information for 2019." https://www.ssa.gov/cola/.

[26] Social Security Administration. "Retirement Planner: Benefits For Your Spouse." https://www.ssa.gov/planners/retire/applying6.html.

date possible, her monthly benefits will be reduced by 67.5 percent, to $520 per month (remember, at FRA, the most she can qualify for is half of Peter's FRA benefit).

What if Peter and Mary Jane both wait until FRA? At sixty-six, Peter begins taking his full benefit of $1,600 a month. Two years later, when she reaches age sixty-six, Mary Jane will qualify for $800 a month. By waiting until FRA, the couple's monthly benefit goes from $1,720 to $2,400.

What if Peter delays until age seventy to get his maximum possible benefit? For each year past FRA that he delays, his monthly benefits increase by 8 percent. This means that, at seventy, he could file for a monthly benefit of $2,112. However, delayed retirement credits do not affect spousal benefits, so as soon as Peter files at seventy, Mary Jane would also file (at age sixty-eight) for her maximum benefit of $800, so their highest possible combined monthly check is $2,912.[27]

When it comes to your Social Security benefits, you obviously will want to consider whether a monthly check based on a fraction of your spouse's earnings will be comparable to or larger than your own earnings history.

I've thrown a lot of numbers at you to consider, like your FRA based on your year of birth, as well as the COLA and spousal benefits (and we haven't even gotten to taxes!), but here's another date to think about: Jan. 2, 1954. What's important about that date, you ask? For those born on or after that date, you can only make the choice to withdraw your benefits one way, one time. That means you will have to pick whether to take a spousal benefit or use your own earnings history, and whichever one you choose will be the check you get every month for the duration of your retirement. However, if you were born BEFORE Jan. 2, 1954, read on.

If you were born before Jan. 2, 1954, you are eligible to change your benefit withdrawal strategy *even after you have*

---

[27] Office of the Chief Actuary. Social Security Administration. "Social Security Benefits: Benefits for Spouses." https://www.ssa.gov/OACT/quickcalc/spouse.html#calculator.

begun withdrawals. This means that you could begin taking a spousal benefit at sixty-two or at FRA while allowing the benefits based on your own earnings history to accrue.[28]

Let's look back to Mary Jane and Peter to see how this could theoretically work. We know that if they both file at FRA, Mary Jane will receive $800 a month when she files, on top of Peter's $1,600 benefit. But what if her own earned credit at FRA was $700? In four years, when Mary Jane turns seventy, the monthly benefit based on her personal earnings will have grown from $700 to $924. At seventy, she could file to trade up her $800 monthly spousal benefit for a $924 monthly check. Remember, this only works for Mary Jane if she was born before Jan. 2, 1954.

Divorced Spouses

There are a few considerations for those of us who have gone through a divorce. If you 1) were married for ten years or more *and* 2) have since been divorced for at least two years *and* 3) are unmarried *and* 4) your ex-spouse qualifies to begin Social Security, you qualify for a spousal benefit based on your ex-husband or ex-wife's earnings history at FRA. A divorced spousal benefit is different from the married spousal benefit in one way: You don't have to wait for your ex-spouse to file before you can file yourself.[29]

For instance, Charles and Moira were married for fifteen years before their divorce, when he was thirty-six and she was forty. Moira has been remarried for twenty years, and, although Charles briefly remarried, his second marriage ended after a few years. Charles' benefits are largely calculated based on his many years of volunteering in schools, meaning his personal monthly benefit is close to zero.

---

[28] Social Security Administration. "Retirement Planner: Benefits For Your Spouse." https://www.ssa.gov/planners/retire/applying6.html.
[29] Social Security Administration. "Retirement Planner: If You Are Divorced." https://www.ssa.gov/planners/retire/divspouse.html.

Although Moira has deferred her retirement, opting to delay benefits until she is seventy, Charles can begin taking benefits calculated from Moira's work history at FRA as early as sixty-two. However, he will also have the option of waiting until FRA to collect the maximum, or 50 percent of Moira's earned monthly benefit at her FRA.

Widowed Spouses

If your marriage ended with the death of your spouse, you might claim a benefit for your spouse's earned income as his or her widow/widower, called a survivor's benefit. Unlike a spousal benefit or divorced benefits, if your husband or wife dies, you can claim his or her full benefit. Also, unlike spousal benefits, if you need to, you can begin taking income when you turn sixty. However, as with other benefit options, your monthly check will be permanently reduced for withdrawing benefits before FRA.

If your spouse began taking benefits before he or she died, you can't delay withdrawing your survivor's benefits to get delayed credits; the Social Security Administration says you can only get as much from a survivor's benefit as your deceased spouse might have gotten, had he or she lived.[30]

Taxes, Taxes, Taxes

With Social Security, as with everything, it is important to consider taxes. It may be surprising, but your Social Security benefits are not tax-free. Despite having been taxed to accrue those benefits in the first place, you may have to pay Uncle Sam income taxes on up to 85 percent of your Social Security.

The Social Security Administration figures these taxes using what they call the provisional income formula. Your provisional income formula differs from the adjusted gross income you use for your regular income taxes. Instead, to find out how much of

---

[30] Social Security Administration. "Benefits Planner: Receiving Survivors Benefits Early."
https://www.ssa.gov/planners/survivors/survivorchartred.html.

your Social Security benefit is taxable, the Social Security Administration calculates it this way:

Provisional Income = Adjusted Gross Income + Nontaxable Interest + ½ of Social Security

See that piece about nontaxable interest? That generally means interest from government bonds and notes. It surprises many people that, although you may not pay taxes on those assets, their income will count against you when it comes to Social Security taxation.

Once you have figured out your provisional income (also called "combined income"), you can use the following chart to figure out your Social Security taxes.[31]

Taxes on Social Security		
Provisional Income = Adjusted Gross Income + Nontaxable Interest + ½ of Social Security		
If you are ___ and your provisional income is ___, then ...		Uncle Sam will tax ___ of your Social Security
Single	Married, filing jointly	
Less than $25,000	Less than $32,000	0%
$25,000 to $34,000	$32,000 to $44,000	Up to 50%
More than $34,000	More than $44,000	Up to 85%

This is one more reason it may be to your advantage to work with financial and tax professionals: They can look at your entire

---

[31] Social Security Administration. "Benefits Planner: Income Taxes and Your Social Security Benefit." https://www.ssa.gov/planners/taxes.html.

financial picture to make your overall retirement approach as tax efficient as possible—including your Social Security benefit.

Working and Social Security: The Earnings Test

If you haven't reached FRA, but you started your Social Security benefits and are still working, things get a little hairy.

Because you have started Social Security payments, the Social Security Administration will pay out your benefits (at that reduced rate, of course, because you haven't reached your FRA). Yet, because you are working, the organization must also withhold from your check to add to your benefits, which you are already collecting. See how this complicates matters?

To straighten the situation, the government has what is called the earnings test. For 2020, you can earn up to $18,240 without it affecting your Social Security check. But for every $2 you earn past that amount; the Social Security Administration will withhold $1. The earnings test loosens in the year of your FRA; if you are reaching FRA in 2020, you can earn up to $48,600 before you run into the earnings test, and the government only withholds $1 for every $3 past that amount. The month you will reach FRA, you are no longer subject to any earnings withholding. For instance, if you are still working and will turn sixty-six on December 28, 2020, you would only have to worry about the earnings test until December, and then you can ignore it entirely. Keep in mind, the money the government withholds from your Social Security benefits while you are working before FRA will be tacked back onto your benefits check after FRA.[32]

In addition, it's important to understand what happens upon the first death of two spouses who are both collecting Social Security. The surviving spouse may elect to receive their

---

[32] Social Security Administration. "Exempt Amounts Under the Earnings Test." https://www.ssa.gov/oact/cola/rtea.html.

deceased spouses' social security if it is greater than their own. The lesser of the two income benefits will be lost.

Postponing Social Security benefits will create greater survivor income for widows. This is a useful strategy for some who either don't need the income right away or who have health issues that may affect their longevity.

CHAPTER SIX

401(k)s & IRAs

Have you heard? Today's retirement is not your parents' retirement. You see, back in the day, it was pretty common to work for one company for the vast majority of your career and then retire with a gold watch and a pension.

The gold watch was a symbol of the quality time you had put in at that company.

The pension was more than a symbol. Instead, it was a guarantee—as solid as your employer—that they would repay your hard work with a certain amount of income in your old age. Did you see that caveat there? Your pension's guarantee was *as solid as your employer.* The problem was, what if your employer went under?

Companies that failed couldn't pay their retired employees' pensions, leading to financial challenges for many. Beginning in 1974 with Congress' passage of the Employee Retirement Income Security Act, federal legislation and regulations aimed at protecting retirees were everywhere, including a relatively obscure section of the Internal Revenue Code, added in 1978. Section 401(k), to be specific.

IRC section 401, subsection k, created tax advantages for employer-sponsored financial products, even if the main contributor was the employee him or herself. Over the years, more employers took note, beginning an age of transition away from pensions and toward 401(k) plans. A 401(k) is a retirement account that has certain tax benefits and restrictions on the investments or other financial products inside of it.

Essentially, 401(k)s and their individual retirement account (IRA) counterparts are "wrappers" that provide tax benefits around other assets; typically, the assets that compose IRAs and 401(k)s are mutual funds, stock and bond mixes, and money market accounts. However, IRA and 401(k) contents are becoming more diverse these days, with some companies offering different kinds of annuity options within their plans.

Where pensions are defined-*benefit* plans, 401(k)s and their individual retirement account (IRA) counterparts are defined-*contribution* plans. That one-word change outlines the basic difference. Pensions spell out what you can expect to receive from the plan but not necessarily how much money it will take to fund those benefits. With 401(k)s, an employer sets a standard for how much they will contribute (if any), and you can be certain of what you are contributing, but there is no outline for what you can expect to receive in return for those contributions.

Modern employment looks very different these days. A 2018 survey by the Bureau of Labor Statistics determined that U.S. workers stayed with their employers a median of about four years. Workers ages 55 to 64 had a little more staying power and were most likely to stay with their employer for about 10 years.[33] Additionally, the outlook on the benefits front is different today, too. In 1979, 38 percent of workers had pensions. But 401(k)s are rising in number, with about 55 million American workers enrolled in a plan.[34]

A far cry from a pension and gold watch, wouldn't you say?

If there is anything to learn from this paradigm shift, it's that you must look out for yourself. Whether you have worked for a company for two years or twenty, you are still the one who has to look out for your own best interests. That holds doubly true

---

[33] Bureau of Labor Statistics. September 20,2018. "Employee Tenure Summary." https://www.bls.gov/news.release/tenure.nr0.htm.
[34] Investment Company Institute. December 31, 2018. "Frequently Asked Questions about 401(k) Plan Research." https://www.ici.org/policy/retirement/plan/401k/faqs_401k.

when it comes to preparing for retirement. If you are one of the lucky ones who still has a pension, good for you. But for the rest of us, it is likely that a 401(k)—or possibly one of its nonprofit- or government-sector counterparts, a 403(b) or 457 plan—is one of your biggest assets for retirement.

Some employers offer incentives to contribute to their company plans, like a company match. On that subject, I have one thing to say: DO IT! Nothing in life is free, as they say, but a company match on your retirement funds is about as close to free money as it gets. If you can make the minimum to qualify for your company's match at all, go for it.

Now, it's likely that during our working years, we mostly "set and forget" our 401(k) funding. Because it is tax-advantaged, your employer is taking money from your paycheck—before taxes—and putting it into your plan for you. Maybe you got to pick a selection of investments, or maybe your company only offers one choice of investment in your 401(k). But when you are ready to retire or move jobs, you have choices to make that require a little more thought and care.

When you are ready to part ways with your job, you have a few options:

- Leave the money where it is
- Take the cash (and pay income taxes and perhaps a 10 percent additional federal tax if you are younger than age fifty-nine-and-one-half)
- Transfer the money to another employer plan (if the new plan allows)
- Roll the money over into a self-directed IRA

Now, these are just general options. You will have to decide, with the help of a financial professional registered to provide investment advice, what's right for you.

Remember what we said earlier about how we change jobs more often these days? That means you likely have a 401(k) with your current company, but you may also have a string of retirement accounts trailing you from other jobs.

When it comes to your retirement income, it's important to be able to pull together ALL your assets, so you can examine what you have and where, and then decide what you will do with it.

Tax-Qualified, Tax-Preferred, Tax-Deferred ... Still TAXED

Financial media often cite IRAs and 401(k)s for their tax benefits. After all, with traditional plans, you put your money in, pre-tax, and it hopefully grows for years, even decades, untaxed. That's why these accounts are called tax-qualified or tax-deferred assets. They aren't TAX-FREE! Rarely does Uncle Sam allow business to go on without receiving his piece of the pie, and your retirement assets are no different. If you didn't pay taxes on the front end, you will pay taxes on the money you withdraw from these accounts in retirement. Don't get me wrong: This isn't an inherently good or bad thing; it's just the way it is. It's important to understand, though, for the sake of planning ahead.

In retirement, many people assume they will be in a lower tax bracket. Are you planning to pare down your lifestyle in retirement? Perhaps you are, and perhaps you will have substantially less income in retirement. But many of my clients tell me they want to live life more or less the same as they always have. The money they would previously have spent on business attire or gas for their commute they now want to spend on hobbies and grandchildren. That's all fine, and for many of them, it is doable, but does it put them in a lower tax bracket? Probably not.

Keep in mind that IRAs, 401(k)s, and their alternatives have a few limitations because of their special tax status. For one thing, the IRS sets limits on your contributions to these retirement accounts. If you are contributing to a 401(k) or an equivalent nonprofit or government plan, your annual contribution limit is $19,500 (as of 2020). If you are fifty or older, the IRS allows additional contributions, called catch-up contributions, of up to $6,500 on top of the regular limit of $19,500. For an IRA, the limit is $6,000, with a catch-up limit of an additional $1,000.[35]

Because their tax advantages come from their intended use for retirement income, withdrawing funds from these accounts before you turn fifty-nine-and-one-half can carry stiff penalties, with a few exceptions. In addition to fees your investment management company might charge, you will have to pay ordinary income taxes AND a 10 percent federal tax penalty.

The fifty-nine-and-one-half rule for retirement accounts is incredibly important to remember, especially when you're young. Many millennials I see in my practice say while they may be socking money away in their workplace retirement plan, that is often the *only* place they are saving. This could be problematic later because of the fifty-nine-and-one-half rule; what if you have an emergency? It is important to fund your retirement, but you need to have access to emergency funds. This can help you avoid breaking into your retirement accounts and incurring taxes and penalties as a result of the fifty-nine-and-one-half rule.

RMDs

Remember how we talked about the 401(k) or IRA being a "tax wrapper" for your funds? Well, eventually, Uncle Sam will want a bite of that candy bar. So, when you turn seventy-two, the government requires you to withdraw a portion of your account, which the IRS calculates based on the size of your account and your estimated lifespan. This required minimum distribution, or RMD, is the government's insurance that it will, at some point, get some taxes from your earnings. Because you didn't pay taxes on the front end, you will now pay income taxes on whatever you withdraw, including your RMDs. Also, let me just remind

---

[35] Troy Segal. Investopedia. January 17, 2020. "What Are the Roth 401(k) Contribution Limits."
https://www.investopedia.com/ask/answers/102714/what-are-roth-401k-contibution-limits.asp

you not to play chicken with the U.S. government; if you don't take your RMDs starting at seventy-two, you will have to write a check to the IRS for 50 PERCENT of the amount of your missed RMDs.

If you don't need income from your retirement accounts, RMDs can seem like more of a tax burden than an income boon. While some people prefer to reinvest their RMDs, this comes with the possibility of additional taxation: You'll pay income taxes on your RMDs and then capital gains taxes on the growth of your investments. If you are legacy minded, there are other ways to use RMDs, many of which have tax benefits.

Permanent Life Insurance

One way to turn those pesky RMDs into a legacy is through permanent life insurance. Assuming you need the death benefit coverage and can qualify for it medically, if properly structured, these products can pass on a sizeable death benefit to your beneficiaries tax-free as part of your general legacy plan.

ILIT

Another way to use RMDs toward your legacy is to work with an estate planning attorney to create an irrevocable life insurance trust (ILIT). This is basically a permanent life insurance policy placed within a trust. Because the trust is irrevocable, you would relinquish control of it, but, unlike with just a permanent life insurance policy, your death benefit won't count toward your taxable estate.

Annuities

Because annuities can be tax-deferred, using all or a portion of your RMDs to fund an annuity contract can be one way to further delay taxation while guaranteeing your income payments (either to you or your loved ones) later. (Assuming you don't need the income from the RMDs during your retirement.)

Qualified Charitable Distributions

If you are charity-minded, you may use your RMDs toward a charitable organization, instead of using them for income. You must do this directly from your retirement account (you can't take the RMD check and *then* pay the charity) for your withdrawals to be qualified charitable distributions (QCDs), but this is one way of realizing some of the benefits of a charitable legacy during your own lifetime. You will not need to pay taxes on your QCDs, and they won't count toward your annual charitable tax deduction limit, plus you'll be able to see how the organization you are supporting uses your donations.

Roth IRA

Since the Taxpayer Relief Act of 1997, there has been a different kind of retirement account, or "tax wrapper," available to the public: the Roth. Roth IRAs and Roth 401(k)s each differ from their traditional counterparts in one big way, which is that you pay your taxes on the front end. This means once your post-tax money is in the Roth account, as long as you follow the rules and limitations of that account, your distributions are truly tax-free. You won't pay income tax when you take withdrawals, so, in turn, you don't have to worry about RMDs. However, Roth accounts have the same limitations as traditional 401(k)s and IRAs when it comes to withdrawing money before age fifty-nine-and-one-half.

Taking Charge

As mentioned earlier, the 401(k) and IRA have largely replaced pensions, but they aren't an equal trade.

Pensions are employer-funded; the money that goes into them is money that wouldn't ever show up on your pay stub. Because 401(k)s are self-funded, you must actively and consciously save. This distinction has made a difference when it comes to funding retirement.

According to one NerdWallet article, the average 401(k) balance for a person age sixty to sixty-nine is $198,600, but the median likely tells the full story. The median 401(k) balance for a person age sixty to sixty-nine is $63,000. The article also cites the general suggestion to aim by age 30 to have saved up an amount equal to 5o percent to 100 percent of your annual salary.[36] For some thirty-year-old's, saving half an annual salary by age thirty is more than some sixty-to-sixty-nine-year-olds have saved for their entire lives.

There can be many reasons why people underfund their retirement plans, like being overwhelmed by the investment choices or taking withdrawals from IRAs when they leave an employer, but the reason at the top of the list is this: People simply aren't participating to begin with.

So, no matter where you're saving, the most important retirement income decision you can make is to sock away your money in the first place.

---

[36] Arielle O'Shea. Nerd Wallet. January 24, 2019. "The Average 401(k) Balance by Age." https://www.nerdwallet.com/article/investing/the-average-401k-balance-by-age

CHAPTER SEVEN

Annuities

In my practice, I offer my clients a variety of insurance products, all designed to help them reach their financial goals. You may be wondering: Why single out a single product in this book?

Well, while most of my clients have a pretty good understanding of business and finance, I sometimes find those who have the impression there must be magic involved. Some people assume there is a magic finance wand we can wave to change years' worth of savings into a strategy for retirement income. But it's not as easy as a goose laying golden eggs or the Fairy Godmother turning a pumpkin into a coach!

Finances aren't magic; it takes lots of hard work and, typically, several financial products and strategies to pull together a complete retirement strategy. Of all the financial products I work with, it seems people find none more mysterious than annuities. And, if I may say, even some of those who recognize the word "annuity" have a limited understanding of the product. So, in the interest of demystifying annuities, let me tell you a little about what an annuity is.

In general, insurance is a financial hedge against risk. Car owners buy auto insurance to protect their finances in case they injure someone or someone injures them. Homeowners have house insurance to protect their finances in case of a fire, flood, or another disaster. People have life insurance to protect their finances in case of untimely death. Almost juxtaposed to life insurance, people have annuities in case of a long life; annuities can give you financial protection by providing consistent and reliable income payments.

The basic premise of an annuity is that you, the annuitant, pay an insurance company some amount in exchange for their contractual guarantee that they will pay you income for a certain time period. How that company pays you, for how long, and how much are all determined by the annuity contract you enter with the insurance company.

How You Get Paid

There are two ways for an annuity contract to provide income: The first is through what is called annuitization, and the second is through the use of income riders. We'll get into income riders in a bit, but let's talk about annuitization. That nice long word is, in my opinion, one reason annuities have a reputation for mystery and misinformation.

Annuitization

When someone "annuitizes" a contract, it is the point where he or she turns on the income stream. Once a contract has been annuitized, there is no going back. If the policyholder lives longer than the insurance company planned, the insurance company is still obligated to pay him or her, even if the payments end up being way more than the contract's actual value. If, however, the policyholder dies an untimely death, depending on the contract type, the insurance company may keep anything left of the money that funded the annuity—nothing would be paid out to the contract holder's survivors. You see where that could make some people balk?

At a high level, here's how it looks from the insurance company's side: Imagine the company has a "pie" of ten people, who all buy contracts at the same time. In the beginning, ten people receive income paid out by the company. A few, let's say three, die earlier. Their remaining contract values are pooled back into the rest of the insurance company's pie. As the others age, they too die, many of them breaking even, with their pieces of the pie reaching zero around the time they pass away. One or two people live well past the others, and, by the time they pass away, they have long since hit zero on the values of their contracts. The insurance company was still able to pay them their contractually agreed income and combined with the investment earnings they gained by investing the premiums they receive from policy holders.

Now, I use this pie illustration to show you the original concept of annuitization and how it works, from the perspectives of both an insurer and a contract holder. Modern annuities have so many bells and whistles that the picture I just described seems too simplified to do them justice, but it's important to at least have a basic concept of annuitization.

Riders

Remember what I said about bells and whistles? Modern annuities have a lot of different options these days, many in the form of riders that are built in for no fee or that you can add to your contract for a fee—usually about 1 percent of the contract value per year. Each rider has its particulars, and the types of riders available will vary by the type of annuity contract purchased, but just to outline some of these little extras:

- Lifetime income rider: Contract guarantees you an enhanced income for life
- Death benefit rider: Contract pays an enhanced death benefit to your beneficiaries even if you have annuitized
- Return of premium rider: Guarantees that you (or your beneficiaries) will at least receive back the premium value of the annuity
- Long-term care rider: Provides a certain amount, sometimes doubling the payout rate of the annuity, to help pay for long-term care for a defined period of time

if the contract holder is moved to a nursing home or assisted living situation

This isn't an extensive look, and usually the riders have fancier names based on the issuing company, like Lorem Ipsum Insurance Company Income Preferred Bonus Fixed Index Annuity rider, but I just wanted to show you what some of the general options are in layperson's terms.

Types of Annuities

Annuities break down into four basic types: immediate, variable, fixed, and fixed index.

Immediate

Immediate annuities primarily rely on annuitization to provide income—you give the insurance company a lump sum up front, and your payments begin immediately. Once you begin receiving income payments, the transaction is irreversible and you no longer have access to your money in a lump sum. When you die, any remaining contract value is typically forfeited to the insurance company.

All other annuity contract types are "deferred" contracts, meaning you fund your policy as a lump sum or over a period of years and you give it the opportunity to grow over time— sometimes years, sometimes decades.

Variable

A variable annuity is an insurance contract as well as an investment. It's sold by insurance companies, but only through someone who is registered to sell investment products. With a variable annuity contract, you are indirectly invested in the stock market. This makes it a bit different from the other annuity contract types because it is the only contract in which your money is subject to losses because of market declines. Your contract value has a greater opportunity to grow, but it also stands to lose. Additionally, your contract's value will be subject to the underlying investment's fees and limitations—including capital gains taxes, management fees, etc. Once it is time for you to receive income from the contract, the insurance company will pay you a certain income, locked in at whatever your contract's value was.

Many insurance companies offer variable annuities that guarantee lifetime income, but the account value of these annuities can grow and lose money because it is invested into the stock market. The annual fees from the top variable annuity contracts tend to range from 3 percent to 5 percent annually, so you generally need to see a substantial annual return to pay the annuity fees and still grow your value. Because of this and their inherent market risk, they are often not suitable products for those in or near retirement.

Fixed

A traditional fixed annuity is pretty straightforward. You purchase a contract with a guaranteed interest rate and, when you are ready, the insurance company will make regular income payments to you at whatever payout rate your contract guarantees. Those payments will continue for the rest of your life and, if you choose, for the remainder of your spouse's life.

Fixed annuities don't have much in the way of upside potential, but many people like them for their guarantees (after all, if your Aunt May lives to be ninety-five, knowing she has a paycheck later in life can be her mental and financial safety net) as well as for their predictability. Unlike variable annuities, which are subject to market risk and might be up one year and down the next, you can easily calculate the value of your fixed annuity over your lifetime.

Fixed Indexed Annuity

To recap, variable annuities take on more risk to offer more possibilities to grow. Fixed annuities have less potential growth, but they protect your principal. In the last couple of decades, many insurance companies have retooled their product line to offer fixed index annuities, which are sort of midway between variable and fixed annuities on that risk/reward spectrum. Fixed index annuities offer greater growth potential than traditional fixed annuities but less than variable annuities. Like traditional fixed annuities, however, fixed index annuities are protected from downside market losses.

Fixed index annuities are market-linked contracts. This means that instead of your contract value growing at a set interest rate like a traditional fixed annuity, it has the potential to grow within a range. Your contract value is credited interest based on the performance of an external market index like the S&P 500, without ever actually being invested in the market. You don't invest in the S&P 500 directly, but the insurance company will credit your annuity contract based on the S&P 500's gains, up to a cap, after a spread, or with a participation rate. For instance, if your contract caps your interest at 5 percent, then in a year that the S&P 500 gains 3 percent as of your annuity anniversary, your annuity value increases 3 percent. If the S&P 500 gains 20 percent, your annuity value gets a 5 percent bump.

If your contract has a spread of 3 percent and the index gains 20 percent as of your anniversary, your annuity value increases 17 percent. If your contract has a 50 percent participation rate and the index earns 10 percent, your annuity value will receive 5 percent. You may change your interest crediting allocations annually on your contract anniversary or elect a combination of index methods each year. Once your interest is credited, it is locked in and can't go down due to market volatility or market losses. This provides principal protection and protects your credited interest from loss.

So, *remember*, since your money isn't actually invested in the market with a fixed index annuity, if the market nosedives (2000 and 2008, anyone?), while you won't see any increase in your contract value, there will also be no decrease in your contract value. No matter how badly the market performed, you won't lose any of the interest you were credited in previous years due to market loss.

So, what if the S&P 500 shows a market loss of 30 percent? Your contract value isn't going anywhere (unless you purchased an optional rider – this charge will still come out of your annuity value each year). For those who are interested in protection with growth potential, fixed index annuities can be an attractive option because, when the stock market has a long period of positive performance, a fixed index annuity can earn greater interest, even potentially offsetting the effects of inflation. And during stretches when the stock market is erratic, and stock values across the board take significant losses? Fixed index annuities won't lose anything due to stock market volatility and won't have to recover from losses. This means the annuity account value can grow from its principal and step up interest if the stock market recovers from its losses.

At Sweitzer Income Planning, LLC, our first meeting with new clients includes both spouses and us in our conference room listening, asking questions, and listening some more. As we listen, we often hear concerns about risk, paying high fees, future long-term healthcare costs, running out of money, financial security for spouses and children, a need for lifetime monthly paychecks in retirement, and financial stress.

When it makes sense for the individual client, we might offer a fixed indexed annuity (FIA) to help our clients protect a portion of the money they don't want at risk in the stock market. Our company is totally independent and represents hundreds of insurance companies to find the appropriate fixed indexed annuities for our clients.

Other Things to Know About Annuities

We just talked about the four kinds of annuity contracts available, but all of them have some commonalities as annuities.

For all annuities, the contractual guarantees are only as strong as the insurance company that sells the product, which makes it important to thoroughly check the credit ratings of any company whose products you are considering.

Annuities are tax-deferred, meaning you don't have to pay taxes on interest earnings each year as the contract value grows. Instead, you will pay ordinary income taxes on your withdrawals. These are meant to be long-term products, so, like other tax-deferred or tax-advantaged products, if you begin taking withdrawals from your contract before age fifty-nine-and-one-half, you may have to pay a 10 percent federal tax penalty. Also, while annuities are generally considered illiquid, most contracts allow you to withdraw up to 10 percent of your contract value every year. Withdraw any more, however, and you could incur additional surrender penalties.

Keep in mind, your withdrawals will deplete the accumulated cash value, death benefit, and possibly the rider values of your contract.

Annuities aren't for everyone, but it's important to understand them before saying "yea" or "nay" on whether they fit in your plan; otherwise you're not operating with complete information, wouldn't you agree? Regardless, you should talk to a financial professional who can help you understand annuities, help you dissect your particular financial needs and show you whether an annuity is appropriate for your retirement income plan.

CHAPTER EIGHT

Estate & Legacy

In my practice, I devote a significant portion of my time to estate matters. That doesn't mean drawing up wills or trusts or putting together powers of attorney or anything like that.

After all, I'm not an estate planning attorney. But I am a financial professional, and what part of the "estate" isn't affected by money matters?

I've included this chapter because I have seen people do estate planning wrong. Clients, or clients' families, have come in after a death in the family and have found themselves in the middle of probate, or high taxes, or have discovered that something unforeseen (often long-term care) drained the estate.

I have also seen people do estate planning right: clients or families who visit my office to talk about legacies and how to make them last, adult children who have room to grieve without an added burden of unintended costs, without stress from a family ruptured because of inadequate planning.

I'll share some of these stories here. However, I'm not going to give you specific advice since everyone's situation is unique. I only want to give you some things to think about and to underscore the importance of planning ahead.

You Can't Take It With You

When it comes to legacy and estate planning, the mostherited assets may also be tied up in probate important thing is to DO IT. I have heard people from clients to celebrities (rap artist

Snoop Dogg comes to mind) who say they aren't interested in what happens to their assets when they die because they'll be dead. That's certainly one way to look at it. But I think that's a very selfish way to go about things—we all have people and causes we care about, and those who care about us. Even if the people we love don't *need* what we leave behind, they can still be fined or legally tied up in the probate process or burial costs if we don't plan for those. And that's not even considering what happens if you become incapacitated at some point while you are still alive. Having a plan in place can greatly reduce the stress of those responsibilities on your loved ones; it's just a loving thing to do.

Life insurance and annuity death benefits can bypass probate if paid directly to properly designated beneficiaries by contract. The beneficiaries must be already properly designated. We provide beneficiary designation reviews as part of our complimentary life and annuity contract reviews. With designations in place, the issuing companies pay the death benefits to the beneficiaries in just a couple of weeks after the owner's death, and they avoid being tied up for a year or two in costly probate.

In many cases, life insurance is one of the best ways to transfer tax-free death benefits to your widow or children at a time when they may need it most. The lump sum death benefits arrive in a timely manner and provide financial assurance so surviving families can properly grieve without dealing with stressful financial issues.

The death benefits can even provide financial comfort to any of your surviving dependents after your death. These benefits can also be payable to grandchildren, nieces, nephews, trusts, business partners, charities, etc…

Tax-free life insurance death benefits are unlike any other financial instrument because of their favorable tax treatment. The total death benefits paid to a beneficiary can be received, invested, spent, or repositioned with no tax (although your estate itself may still be subject to estate taxes). Conversely, inherited IRAs, 401(k)s, and pensions can retain their tax status if transferred directly into the beneficiaries' own IRA account (when permitted), but the government taxes all current and future withdrawals as ordinary income in the tax year they are received.

These inherited IRAs and 401(k)s can be tied up in probate, too. They are also subject to the new Secure Act's "ten-year rule," enacted January 1, 2020. Those who inherit IRAs or 401(k)s must liquidate and pay taxes on these accounts within ten years of the date of death of the deceased unless they qualify for an exemption, such as being the surviving spouse, a disabled child, etc. Your estate planning attorney can help you decide which beneficiary designation might make the most sense for you.

Documents

There are a few documents that lay the groundwork of legacy planning. You've probably heard of all or most of them, but I'd like to review what they are and how people commonly use them. These are all things you should talk about with an estate planning attorney to establish your legacy.

Powers of Attorney

A power of attorney, or POA, is a document that gives someone the authority to act on your behalf, in your best interests. These come in handy in situations where you cannot be present (think vacation where you get stuck in Canada) or, for durable powers of attorney, even when you are incapacitated (think in a coma or coping with dementia).

It is important to have powers of attorney in place and to appoint someone you trust to act on your behalf in these matters. Have you ever heard of someone who was incapacitated after a car accident, whether from head trauma or being in a coma for weeks—sometimes months? Do you think their bills stopped coming due during that time? I like my phone company and my bank, but neither one is about to put a moratorium on sending me bills, particularly not for an extended or interminable period. A power of attorney would have the authority to make sure your mortgage gets paid or cancel your cable while you are unable.

You can have multiple POAs and require them to act jointly.

What this looks like: Do you think two heads are better than one? One man, Chris, greatly relied on his two sons' opinions for both his business and personal matters. He appointed both sons as joint POA, requiring both their signoffs for his medical and financial matters.

You can have multiple POAs who can act independently.

What this looks like: Irene had three children with whom she routinely stayed. They lived in different areas of the country, which she thought was an advantage; one month she might be hiking out West, the next she could enjoy the newest off-Broadway production, and the next she could soak up some Southern sun. She named her three children as independently authorized POAs so, if something happened, no matter where she was, the child closest could step in to act on her behalf.

You can have POAs who have different responsibilities.

What this looks like: Although Luke's friend Claire, a nurse, was his go-to and POA for health-related issues, financial matters usually made her nervous, so he appointed his good neighbor, Matt, as his POA in all of his financial and legal matters.

In addition to POAs, it may be helpful to have an advance medical directive. This is a document in which you have pre-decided what choices you would make about different health scenarios. An advance medical directive can help ease the burden for your medical POA and loved ones, particularly when it comes to end-of-life care.

Wills

Perhaps the most basic document of legacy planning, a will is a legal document wherein you outline your wishes for your estate. When it comes to your estate after your death, having a will is the foundation of your legacy. Without one, your loved ones are left behind, guessing what you would have wanted, and the court will largely split your assets according to the state's defaults. And maybe that's exactly what you wanted, as far as anyone knows, right? Because even if you told your nephew that he could have your car he's been driving, if it's not in writing, it still might go to the brother, sister, son, or daughter to whom you aren't speaking.

However, it may not be enough just to have a will. Even with a will, your assets will be subject to probate. Probate is what we call the state's process for determining a will's validity. A judge will go through your will to question if it is in conflict with state law, if it is the most up-to-date document, if you were mentally competent at the time it was in order, etc. For some, this is a quick, easily resolved process. For others, particularly if someone steps forward to contest the will, it may take years to settle, all the while subjecting their assets to court costs and attorney's fees.

One other undesirable piece of the probate process is that it is a public process. That means anyone can go to the courthouse, ask for copies of the case, and find out your assets. They can also see who is slated to receive what and who is disputing.

It's also important to remember that beneficiary lines trump wills. So, that large life insurance policy? What if, when you bought it fifteen years ago, you wrote your ex-husband's name on the beneficiary line? Even if you stipulate otherwise in your will, the company that holds your policy will pay out to your ex-spouse. Or, how about the thousands of dollars in your IRA you dedicated to the children thirty years ago, but one of your children was killed in a car accident, leaving his wife and two toddlers behind? That IRA is going to transfer to your remaining children, with nothing for your daughter-in-law and grandchildren.

That may paint a grim portrait, but I can't underscore enough the importance of working with a skilled estate planning attorney to keep your will and beneficiary lines up to date as your life changes, for the sake of your loved ones.

People who do their own estate planning ineffectively can run into trouble because they try to do it on their own. Unless told explicitly, they do not realize what they did wrong until the wrath is felt by their family members and beneficiaries after they die. To all the people who are trying to plan their estate on their own, your family may pay the price.

We saw this unfold firsthand with Cari's father. He successfully ran his family business for forty-five years. He was confident in himself as a father, businessman, and planner. He was always resistant to talk to Cari about the plan and actual position of his estate. It was not until after he died last year that we found out he did not have as much control as he thought he did. That does not in any way mean he did not have the best intentions to leave his estate better off for his wife. It means he had a little too much pride in handling everything on his own.

Financial security is a hard thing to master. Thirty-eight years in the business and I still am learning. Seeking professional help can increase the confidence and clarity about what you will be leaving behind to your loved ones.

Trusts

Another piece of legacy planning to consider is the trust.

A trust is set up through an attorney and allows a third party, or trustee, to hold your assets and determine how they will pass to your beneficiaries. Many people are skeptical of trusts because they assume trusts are only appropriate for the fabulously wealthy.

However, a simple trust may only cost around $1,000 to $2,500 in attorney's fees[37] and can avoid both the expense and publicity of probate, provide a more immediate transfer of wealth, avoid some taxes, and provide you greater control of your legacy.

For instance, if you want to set aside some funds for a grandchild's college education, you can make it a requirement that he or she enrolls in classes before your trust will dispense any funds. Like a will, beneficiary lines will override your trust conditions, so you must still keep insurance policies and other assets up to date.

Like any financial or legal consideration, there are many options these days beyond the simple yes/no question of whether to have a trust. For one thing, you will need to consider if you want your trust to be revocable (you can change the terms while you are alive) or irrevocable (can't be changed; you are no longer the "owner" of the contents). A brief note here about irrevocable trusts: Although they have significant and greater tax benefits, they are still subject to a Medicaid look-back period. This means, if you transfer your assets into an irrevocable trust in an attempt to shelter them from a Medicaid spend-down, you will be ineligible for Medicaid coverage for long-term care for five years. Yet, an irrevocable trust can avoid both probate and estate taxes, and it can even protect assets from legal judgments against you.

Another thing to remember when it comes to trusts, in general, is that even if you have set up a trust, you must remember to fund it. In my thirty-eight years' work, I've had numerous clients come to me, assuming they have protected their assets with a trust. When we talk about taxes and other pieces of their legacy, it turns out they never retitled any assets or changed any paperwork on the assets they wanted in the trust.

---

[37] Regan Rondinelli-Haberek. LegalZoom. "What is the Average Cost to Prepare a Living Trust?" https://info.legalzoom.com/average-cost-prepare-living-trust-26932.html.

So please remember, a trust is just a bunch of fancy legal papers if you haven't followed through on retitling your assets.

Taxes

Although charitable contributions, trusts, and other tax-efficient strategies can reduce your tax bill, it's unlikely that your estate will be passed on entirely tax-free. Yet, when it comes to building a legacy that can last for generations, taxes can be one of the biggest drains on the impact of your hard work.

For 2017, the federal estate exemption was $5.49 million per individual and $10.98 million for a married couple, with estates facing up to a 40 percent tax rate after that. For 2020, those limits increased to $11.58 million for individuals and $23.16 million for married couples, with the 40 percent top level gift and estate tax remaining the same. Currently, the new estate limits are set to increase with inflation until January 1, 2026, when they will "sunset" back to the inflation-adjusted 2017 limits.[38] [39] And that's not taking into account the various state regulations and taxes regarding estate and inheritance transfers.

One "frequent flyer" on the tax list: retirement accounts.

Your IRA or 401(k) can be a source of tax issues when you pass away. For one thing, taking funds from a sizable account can trigger a large tax bill. However, if you leave the assets in the account, whoever inherits the IRA will still pay income taxes on those assets. If you pass the account to your spouse, he or she can retitle the account in his or her name and receive RMDs based on his or her life expectancy. Remember, if you don't take your RMDs, the IRS will take up to 50 percent of whatever your

---

[38] Ashlea Ebeling. Forbes. December 21, 2018. "Final Tax Bill Includes Huge Estate Tax Win for the Rich: The $22.4 Million Exemption." https://www.forbes.com/sites/ashleaebeling/2017/12/21/final-tax-bill-includes-huge-estate-tax-win-for-the-rich-the-22-4-million-exemption/.

[39] Ashlea Ebeling. Forbes. November 6, 2019. "IRS Announces Higher Estate And Gift Tax Limits For 2020." https://www.forbes.com/sites/ashleaebeling/2019/11/06/irs-announces-higher-estate-and-gift-tax-limits-for-2020/#18b9e5652efb

required distribution was, plus you will still have to pay income taxes whenever you withdraw that money. However, if you are single, divorced, or widowed, or your surviving spouse will simply not need the money, you can leave the retirement account to someone else, but, with few exceptions (if they are fewer than ten years younger or if they are a disabled child), any non-spouse beneficiaries will have to withdraw all funds from the account within ten years of your passing.

CHAPTER NINE

Women-Specific Concerns
with Cari Sweitzer

I help men, women, and families from all walks of life on their journey to and through retirement. Yet, I want to address the female demographic specifically. Why? To be perfectly blunt, women are more likely than men to deal with poverty when they reach retirement. One report notes that nearly two-thirds of the 7.1 million older adults living in poverty in the United States are women.[40]

The topics, products, and strategies I cover throughout this book are meant to help address retirement concerns for men and women, but those kinds of statistics are a reminder that much of traditional planning is geared toward men. Male careers, male lifespans, male health care. Women's career paths often look much different than men's, so why would their retirement strategies look the same?

This is why I am so grateful to work with my wife, Cari. It is my pleasure to allow her to share her story with you throughout this chapter.

---

[40] Liz Seggert. Association of Health Care Journalists. January 8, 2019. "New Report Paints a Grim Picture of Older Women in Poverty." https://healthjournalism.org/blog/2019/01/new-report-paints-a-grim-picture-of-older-women-in-poverty/.

CARI SWEITZER:

Have you ever received a phone call that just blindsides you? A phone call that changes your life and the way you operate? That call happened for me on May 9, 2018. It was one of the most difficult years of my life, yet it was one I wouldn't change for anything. My dad called me to say the doctor saw something on an ultrasound they wanted to take a closer look at. He had gone in because he had a kidney stone, and they wanted to make sure it had passed. He looked and felt great and was still working at his family business after forty-five years. About a month later, my dad and I went to a urologist who told us he still saw little growths on his bladder. They wanted to scrape it out and see what was going on. No big deal, right? Turns out, it was a huge deal. My dad was immediately diagnosed with bladder cancer. Thus began my family's journey. In and out of the hospital, my dad had surgery to remove the bladder, underwent intense chemotherapy, and even experienced failing kidneys. Ladies, you all know who became my father's nurse through all that, right? Me!

How did that job land on me? Well, my mom doesn't drive into New Haven (it's too confusing for her), and my two brothers were busy running our family business. So all of his care fell on me. Don't get me wrong, I was happy to take on the job. It just put a lot of strain on my work and on my own family.

During this time, I would talk to my dad about what the future would look like. He was always positive that things would eventually return to normal. I felt bad pressing him on things like "how much money will Mom have" or "what kind of pension will she receive after you pass?" I asked passively, and he would just reply, "Your mom will be fine."

Less than a year later, I sat in the hospital with my dad when he made the brave decision to not have any more surgeries or treatments. His body had just grown so weak from the cancer's constant beatings. We set up hospice to come to the house, and I spoke with his doctors daily. They said his blood work was good for the time, but, once it got knocked out of whack again, he would have about twenty-four to forty-eight hours left to live.

We didn't know how long it would take for the imbalance to begin, so we came home and basically prepared for life without Dad. Even with the preparation, I really don't think he or my mom grasped what was happening.

As a very organized person, I had already bought my dad a Father's Day gift. I told my family we were switching Mother's Day and Father's Day that year, and the response I got from my parents and brothers was, "Why? You don't expect dad to be around?" I knew my dad wasn't going to be with us, but the rest of my family just couldn't grasp it. He died May 19, 2019, only one week after our last—early—Father's Day. I tell you this because my dad knew he was going to die. I did as well, and yet no one was asking the tough questions. I tried, but my mother and brothers made me feel like I was rushing his death and being insensitive.

I tried to explain that we needed to know things, like how much money is in his IRA? Does his pension pass on to Mom? Where are the safety deposit keys? Where are the wills? I got a few of the answers from my dad but not enough. After his death we, unfortunately, found my dad's IRA was in just a few stocks that were bleeding money. He had done all his financial planning himself, and he was a very private person. Worst of all, his pension died with him. My mom was left with a little bit of savings, little IRA money, and a nice house that had been paid off until my father had to take a $60,000 home equity line out on it for the family business. I was mad at myself for not pushing harder on him to come clean about his finances.

To this day my mom is still in disbelief as to how he left her needing to sell the house she loves. I tried to warn her we, as women, need to know our financial situations, but it's too late for my mom at this point. For many couples of her generation, that's just how things worked: men took care of the money. She's not alone. Sadly, I've heard this story many times over from the clients I meet.

My mom keeps saying my dad was probably lying in bed dying of guilt knowing what a predicament he was leaving behind. I am not so sure. I don't know if he even knew what his whole financial situation looked like. Notice I didn't say "his *financial plan,*" because he never put a plan together. He just kept saying he was all good. He never took the time to examine the "what if" scenario. I think he felt he could handle it, and maybe he was scared to take a closer look. You've all heard the saying, "people don't plan on failing, they simply fail to plan!" Whatever his reason was, it does my mom no good. It breaks my heart to have seen my mom walk by my dad's picture and say, "look at the mess you put me in."

When the sun sets on your life, are you prepared? When your loved ones tell your story—the story of all the good you did in your life—it is my wish they will talk about how lucky they are you took action when you could and took care of your financial future. Ken is a very supportive husband, but it still is my responsibility to advocate for myself, to intervene, and to understand both of our financial plans. It is crucial for women to understand their finances and to feel empowered to realize they deserve to know. This is why this chapter is so valuable to me. Hopefully it opens women's eyes to their own financial understanding and teaches them the importance of being informed.

Be Informed

It's a familiar scene in many financial offices across the country: A woman comes into an appointment carrying a sack full of unopened envelopes. Often through tears, she sits across the desk from a financial professional and apologizes her way through a conversation about what financial products she owns and where her income is coming from. She is recently widowed and was sure her spouse was taking care of the finances, but now she doesn't know where all their assets are kept, and her confidence in her financial outlook has wavered after walking through funeral expenses and realizing she's down to one income.

Often, she may be financially okay. Yet the uncertainty can be wearying, particularly when the family is already reeling from a loss. While this scenario sometimes plays out with men, too, in my experience, it's more likely to be a woman in that chair across from my desk, probably in part because of Western traditions about money management being "a guy thing." But it doesn't have to be this way. This all-too-common scenario can be wiped away with just a little preparation.

Talk to Your Spouse/ Work with a Financial Professional

While there are many factors that affect women's financial preparation for and situation in retirement, I cannot emphasize enough that the decision to be informed, to be a part of the conversation and to be aware of what is going on with your finances is absolutely paramount to a confident retirement. With all the couples I've seen, there is almost always an "alpha" when it comes to finances. It isn't always men—for many of my coupled clients, the wife is the alpha who keeps the books and budgets and knows where all of the family's assets are down to the penny—yet, statistically among baby boomers, it usually is a man who runs the books. But as time goes on, it looks like the ratio of male to female financial alphas is evening out. According to a Gallup study, women are equally as likely to take the lead on finances as men, with 37 percent of U.S. households showing women primarily paying the bills. Half of households also say decisions about savings and investments are shared equally.[41] Whether that's the way your household works or not, there isn't anything wrong with that. The breakdown happens when there is a lack of communication, when no one other than the financial alpha knows how much the family has and where. In the end, it doesn't matter which person handles the money; it's all about all parties being informed of what's going on financially.

---

[41] Megan Brenan. Gallup. January 29, 2020. "Women Still Handle Main Household Tasks in U.S.." https://news.gallup.com/poll/283979/women-handle-main-household-tasks.aspx

There are a lot of ways to open up the conversation about money. One woman started a conversation with her husband, the financial alpha, by sitting down and saying, "Teach me how to be a widow." Perhaps that sounds grim, but it was to the point, and it spurred what she said was a very fruitful conversation. Couples sometimes have their first real conversation about money, assets, and their retirement plans in our office. The important thing about having these conversations isn't where, it's when . . . and the when is as soon as possible.

Spouse-Specific Options

One area where it might be especially important to be on the same page between spouses is when it comes to financial products or services that have spousal options. A few that come to mind are pensions and Social Security, although life insurance and annuity policies also have the potential to affect both spouses.

With pensions, taking the worker's life-only option is somewhat attractive—after all, the monthly payment is bigger. However, you and your spouse should discuss your options. When we're talking about both of you as opposed to just one lifespan, there is an increased likelihood that at least one of you will live a long, long time. That means the monthly payout will be less, but it also ensures that, no matter which spouse outlives the other, no one will have to suffer the loss of a needed pension paycheck in his or her later retirement years.

While we cover Social Security options in a different chapter, I think some of the spousal information bears repeating. Particularly if you worked exclusively inside the home for a significant number of years, you may want to talk about taking your Social Security benefits based on your spouse's work history. After all, Social Security is based on your thirty-five highest-earning years.

Things to keep in mind about Social Security spousal benefits:[42]

- Your benefit will be calculated as a percentage (up to 50 percent) of your spouse's earned monthly benefit at his or her full retirement age, or FRA.
- For you to begin receiving a spousal benefit, your spouse must have already filed for his or her own benefits, and you must be at least sixty-two.
- You can qualify for a full half of your spouse's benefits if you wait until your FRA to file.
- Beginning your benefits earlier than your FRA will reduce your monthly check, but waiting to file until after FRA will not increase your benefits.

For divorcees: [43]
- You may qualify to withdraw an ex-spousal benefit if
  a. You were married for a decade or more
  b. AND you are at least sixty-two
  c. AND you have been divorced for at least two years
  d. AND you are currently unmarried
  e. AND your ex-spouse is sixty-two (qualifies to begin taking Social Security)
- Your ex-spouse does not have to have filed for you to file on his or her benefit
- Similar to spousal benefits, you can qualify for up to half of your ex-spouse's benefits if you wait to file until your FRA.
- If your ex-spouse dies, you may file to receive a widow/widower benefit on his or her Social Security

---

[42] Social Security Administration. "Retirement Planner: Benefits For You As A Spouse." https://www.ssa.gov/planners/retire/applying6.html.
[43] Social Security Administration. "Retirement Planner: If You Are Divorced." https://www.ssa.gov/planners/retire/divspouse.html.

record as long as you are at least age sixty and fulfill all the other requirements on the preceding alphabetized list.

    a. This will not affect the benefits of your ex-spouse's current spouse

For widow's (or widower's) benefits:[44]
- You may qualify to receive as much as your deceased spouse would have received if . . .
  a. You were married for at least nine months before his or her death
  b. OR you would qualify for a divorced spousal benefit
  c. AND you are at least sixty
  d. AND you did not/have not remarried before age sixty
- You may earn delayed credits IF your spouse hadn't already filed for benefits when he or she died
- Other rules may apply to you if you are disabled or are caring for a deceased spouse's dependent or disabled child

Longevity

On average, women live longer than men. Most stats put average female longevity at about two years more than men's. But averages are tricky things. I think perhaps a more telling statistic is the fact that more than 80 percent of U.S. centenarians, those over 100, are women. That means the vast majority of the oldest old are women.[45]

---

[44] Social Security Administration. "Survivors Planner: If You Are The Worker's Widow Or Widower."
https://www.ssa.gov/planners/survivors/ifyou.html#h2.

[45] U.S. Census Bureau. December 10, 2012. "2010 Census Report Shows More Than 80 Percent of Centenarians are Women."
https://www.census.gov/newsroom/releases/archives/2010_census/cb12-239.html.

On one hand, this is a Rosie the Riveter moment. How fabulous are women? On the other hand, this has longstanding financial ramifications.

Many financial professionals focus mainly on asset accumulation with the breadwinner of the family. At Sweitzer Income Planning, we customize and build our tax-effective income strategies with both spouses in our meetings. It's imperative that women, whether breadwinners or not, have equal input in their income approach. Women's concerns and wants need to be addressed and included in their families' strategies. It is vital both spouses have the financial confidence and comfort to execute their income strategy, even after they become widows.

Achieving financial confidence is often more important to women. By increasing their financial confidence, they protect themselves against the unexpected. Financial confidence is critical to learn before life changes and the unexpected starts to take over. After all, 77.4 percent of women age eighty-five and older will outlive their spouses, eventually placing them solely in charge of their household finances.[46] Without financial confidence, these women are less likely to find themselves in ideal situations.

So, what are we going to do about it? My goal of working with women is to make sure they have a strategy designed to achieve their desired lifestyle in retirement. I want to show them how to guarantee income for life and even how to prepare for retirement on a modest income. At Sweitzer Income Planning, we will listen to your concerns and worries and be open and honest with you. We will respond to you in a timely manner, to not add onto any stress you may be experiencing. We recognize everyone is not financially literate, and we will make sure you leave conversations and meetings more financially knowledgeable and confident. We will make sure you are

---

[46] Medicine Encyclopedia. "The Demography of Widowhood." https://medicine.jrank.org/pages/1840/Widowhood-demography-widowhood.html

understanding what is going on by simply talking *with* you and not *at* you.

Simply Needing More Money in Retirement

Living longer in retirement means needing more money, period. Barring a huge lottery win or some crazy stock market action, the date you retire is likely the point at which you have the most money you will ever have. Not to put too grim a spin on it, but the problem with longevity is that, the further you get away from that date, the further your dollars have to stretch. If you planned to live to a nice eighty-something, but you live to a nice one-hundred-something, that is TWO DECADES you will need to account for, monetarily.

To put this in perspective, let's say you like to drink coffee as an everyday splurge. Not accounting for inflation or leap years, a $2.50 cup-a-day habit is $18,250 over a two-decade span. Now think of all the things you like to do that cost money. Add those up for twenty years of unanticipated costs. I think you'll see what I mean.

More Health Care Needs

In addition to the cost of living for a longer lifespan is the fact that, plain and simple, aging means more health care, and more health care means more money. Women are survivors. They suffer from the morbidity-mortality paradox, which states women suffer more non-fatal illnesses throughout their lifetime than men, who experience fewer illnesses but higher mortality. Men experience less sickness in general, but they are more susceptible to death when they do experience illness.[47] So survival is on the side of the woman. However, surviving things like cancer also means more checkups later in life.

---

[47] Melinda Martin-Khan. Medical Xpress. June 10, 2019. "Why Do Women Live Longer Than Men?" https://medicalxpress.com/news/2019-06-women-longer-men.html

Widowhood

Not only do women typically live longer than their same-age male counterparts, they also have the tendency to marry men older than themselves. The numbers bear this out: women are four times more likely to outlive their spouses than men.[48] In addition, 50 percent of women will become widowed by age sixty-five—and many may live at least another fifteen years or more on their own.[49]

I don't say this to scare people; rather, I think it's fundamentally important to prepare my female clients for something that may be a startling BUT VERY LIKELY scenario. At some point, most women will have to handle their financial situations on their own. A little preparation can go a long way, and having a basic understanding of your household finances and the "who, what, where, and how much" of your family's assets is incredibly useful—and can prevent a tragic situation from being more traumatic.[50]

As if to underscore the point that the financial services industry often underserves women in these situations, consider this statistic: 70 percent of widows fire their financial advisors after their spouses die.[51] In my opinion, this is because many financial professionals tend to alienate women even when their spouses are alive. I've heard several stories of women who sat through meeting after meeting without their financial professional ever addressing a single question to them.

In our firm, when we work with couples, we work hard to make sure our retirement income strategies work for both

---

[48] Women's Institute for A Secure Retirement. 2019. "Widowhood: Why Women need to Talk About This Issue." https://www.wiserwomen.org/resources/widowhood-fact-sheets/widowhood-why-women-need-to-talk-about-this-issue/
[49] Ibid.
[50] Lifetime Financial Growth. June 01, 2019. "Why Are We Unprepared for Widowhood?" https://www.lifetimefinancialgrowth.com/blog/why-are-we-unprepared-for-widowhood
[51] Mercer Partners Wealth Management. September 30, 2019. "Transitions." https://www.mercerpartnerswealth.com/p/transitions

people. No matter who is the financial alpha, it's important for everyone who is affected by a retirement strategy to understand it.

Taxes

One of the aspects of widowhood that often comes unexpectedly is the tax bill. Many women continue similar lifestyles to the ones they shared with their spouses. This, in turn, means continuing to have a similar need for income. However, after the death of a spouse, their taxes will be calculated based on a single filer's income table, which is much less forgiving than the couple's tax rates. With proper planning, your financial professional and tax advisor may be able to help you take the sting out of your new tax status.

Caregiving

Of the 44 million caregivers providing unpaid, informal care for older adults, the majority are women. Most women who provide caregiving services are still in the workforce. Yet, on average, female caregivers lose around $324,044 in wages. This doesn't even account for Social Security benefit losses or the losses of health care benefits and retirement savings.[52] This also doesn't account for maternity care, mothers who homeschool, or women who leave the workforce to care for their children in any way.

I don't repeat these statistics to scare you. Estimates typically place the monetary value of unofficial caregiving services across the United States at around $150 billion or more. Yet, I think the emotional value of care that many women provide their relatives or neighbors cannot be quantified. So, to be clear, this shouldn't be taken as a "why not to provide caregiving." Instead, it should be seen as a call for "why *prepare* for caregiving" or "how to lessen the financial and emotional burden of caregiving."

---

[52] Where You Live Matters. November 5, 2019. "The High Costs of Caring for a Loved One." https://www.whereyoulivematters.org/the-high-costs-of-caring-for-a-loved-one/

To address the issue of caregiving, many insurance companies now provide a great opportunity to purchase permanent or term life insurance policies that include home healthcare and chronic illness riders. If you need the death benefit life insurance offers and are healthy, you may qualify for a new policy with these long-term care benefits. We review your current policies and evaluate if your current coverage still meets your needs and then determine if it may make sense to re-evaluate another policy to purchase these additional benefits

Funding Your Own Retirement

For these reasons, women need to be prepared to fund more of their own retirements. There are several savings options and products, including the spousal 401(k). Unlike a traditional 401(k), where you contribute money to a plan with your employer, a spousal 401(k) is something your spouse sets up on your behalf, so he or she can contribute a portion of the paycheck to your retirement funds. This is something to consider, particularly for families where one spouse has dropped out of the workforce to care for a relative.

Also, if you find yourself in a caregiving role, talk to your employer's human resources department. Some companies have paid leave, special circumstance, or sick leave options that you could qualify for, making it easier to cope and possibly helping you stay in the workforce longer.

Saving Money

Women need more money to fund their retirements, period. But this doesn't have to be a significant burden—most of the time, women are better at saving, investing, and paying down debt.[53] This gives me reason to believe that, as women get more

---

[53] Dori Zinn. Debt.com. December 18, 2018. "Women are Better than Men at Money Management." https://www.debt.com/news/budgeting-saving/handling-money-women-better-money-management/.

involved in their finances, families will continue to be better-prepared for retirement, both HIS and HERS.

CHAPTER TEN

Finding a Financial Professional

Many people experience lots of uncertainty about whether they will have enough money to stop working and when they should retire. This abundance of uncertainty is particularly high today. Many factors out of your control include, but are not limited to, the new tax law limiting the number of deductions the average taxpayer can use in their income tax filing, and the fact we had an eleven-year bull market run before the economy slowed and cooled, with a bear market thanks to coronavirus.[54] What is in your control: day-to-day saving and planning decisions. These factors prove to be the most critical to your retirement success.

Some people may think they can do their financial preparation all by themselves. Today, this can be particularly hard because an income strategy can sometimes be similar to a jigsaw puzzle. You have many pieces that need to fit together to result in the final product you want—a reliable financial strategy. How big each piece is and where it fits all depends on you and your needs. The process to choose and place these pieces is where we come in.

---

[54] Daniel Laboe. NASDAQ.com. March 12, 2020. "Coronavirus Ends Bull-Run." https://www.nasdaq.com/articles/coronavirus-ends-bull-run-2020-03-13

One of the hardest parts of financial preparation is planning for the "income phase" or post-retirement years. In order to have financial confidence throughout retirement, you want to have reliable income flowing in weekly or monthly, backed by principal protection. We refer to this as your retirement "paychecks." To achieve financial longevity, these paychecks must pay you as long as you live. One way to secure lifetime income is by using fixed indexed annuities, life insurance, or the combination of the two, if it makes sense for your unique circumstances. This can help you to retire knowing you will have a regular, guaranteed stream of income during your lifetime.

Statistics show the majority of hiking accidents and injuries happen when hikers are descending from a mountain as opposed to climbing it.[55] This is often because they pay less attention to their footing and surroundings after they have completed the goal of reaching the top of the hike. People lose sight of what follows after crossing the finish line, so we say. This is often the same for financial preparation. People tend to have less financial awareness post-retirement. This is why consulting with a financial professional can be so important.

Funny story: my wife and I took the hiking statistic both seriously and literally. We hiked to the top of Mount Washington with our family and had our son drive us back down in his car! He drove up earlier and hiked down quickly to meet us for the adventure up. Proper planning and execution with the resources of one family member can benefit the whole family. We played it safe and still got the picture to prove we made it to the top.

---

[55] The American Alpine Club. 2018. *Accidents in North American Climbing.*

Acknowledgments

There are many people who contributed to or inspired the content and creation of this book. First and foremost, I would like to thank my family for not only supporting Cari and I throughout the design of the book, but also showing us there is much more than just memories we leave behind after we die. Cari would like to personally thank her dad for teaching her how to handle adversity and death with grace and courage. Ironically, she would also like to thank him for showing her how very important it is to plan financially for your death, even if it was through unfortunate circumstances. Most importantly, he taught her how to live life to its fullest, which she will always be grateful for. We also want to thank Advisors Excel for their support and knowledge in compiling this book. Lastly, we would like to thank all of our clients for trusting us to help with securing their financial future. We do not take the responsibility lightly.

About the Author

Ken Sweitzer and Sweitzer Income Planning, LLC

Ken found his start in the industry in 1982, as a life insurance and annuity specialist with Travelers Life Insurance Company in Hamden, CT. He holds licenses for Life Insurance, Accident, & Health Insurance in District of Columbia, Florida, Maine, Rhode Island, Connecticut, Maryland, Massachusetts, North Carolina, New York, Florida, California, Connecticut, New Jersey, and Michigan. Ken earned a Finance Degree from the University of Connecticut, and he remains one of the most decorated student-athletes in the history of the University of Connecticut Football Program. At UConn he was the four-year starting quarterback and earned All-Yankee Conference Honors six times including Player of the Year in 1981. He competed against Danny White for the quarterback position at the Dallas Cowboys training camp in 1982.

In his free time, Ken enjoys watching movies with his family, hiking, golfing, and spending quality time with his wife of thirty years, Cari, and their three children, KC (twenty-eight), Sam (twenty-five), and Sloane (twenty-two).

Made in the USA
Monee, IL
12 July 2020